Map and T~~erritory~~

Rationality: From A~~I to Zombies~~
Book One

ELIEZER YUDKOWSKY

Written by Eliezer Yudkowsky

Published in 2018 by the
Machine Intelligence Research Institute
Berkeley 94704
United States of America
intelligence.org

Cover artwork and design by Jimmy Rintjema

ISBN-13: 978-1-939311-23-8

FIRST PRINT EDITION

Preface

You hold in your hands a compilation of two years of daily blog posts. In retrospect, I look back on that project and see a large number of things I did completely wrong. I'm fine with that. Looking back and *not* seeing a huge number of things I did wrong would mean that neither my writing nor my understanding had improved since 2009. *Oops* is the sound we make when we improve our beliefs and strategies; so to look back at a time and not see anything you did wrong means that you haven't learned anything or changed your mind since then.

It was a mistake that I didn't write my two years of blog posts with the intention of helping people do better in their everyday lives. I wrote it with the intention of helping people solve big, difficult, important problems, and I chose impressive-sounding, abstract problems as my examples.

In retrospect, this was the second-largest mistake in my approach. It ties in to the *first*-largest mistake in my writing, which was that I didn't realize that the big problem in learning this valuable way of thinking was figuring out how to practice it, not knowing the theory. I didn't realize that part was the priority; and regarding this I can only say "Oops" and "Duh."

Yes, sometimes those big issues really are big and really are important; but that doesn't change the basic truth that to master skills you need to practice them and it's harder to practice on things that are further away. (Today the Center for Applied Rationality is working on repairing this huge mistake of mine in a more systematic fashion.)

A third huge mistake I made was to focus too much on rational belief, too little on rational action.

The fourth-largest mistake I made was that I should have better organized the content I was presenting in the sequences. In particular, I should

i

have created a wiki much earlier, and made it easier to read the posts in sequence.

That mistake at least is correctable. In the present work Rob Bensinger has reordered the posts and reorganized them as much as he can without trying to rewrite all the actual material (though he's rewritten a bit of it).

My fifth huge mistake was that I—as I saw it—tried to speak plainly about the stupidity of what appeared to me to be stupid ideas. I did try to avoid the fallacy known as Bulverism, which is where you *open* your discussion by talking about how stupid people are for believing something; I would always discuss the issue first, and only afterwards say, "And so this is stupid." But in 2009 it was an open question in my mind whether it might be important to have some people around who expressed contempt for homeopathy. I thought, and still do think, that there is an unfortunate problem wherein treating ideas courteously is processed by many people on some level as "Nothing bad will happen to me if I say I believe this; I won't lose status if I say I believe in homeopathy," and that derisive laughter by comedians can help people wake up from the dream.

Today I would write more courteously, I think. The discourtesy did serve a function, and I think there were people who were helped by reading it; but I now take more seriously the risk of building communities where the normal and expected reaction to low-status outsider views is open mockery and contempt.

Despite my mistake, I am happy to say that my readership has so far been amazingly good about *not* using my rhetoric as an excuse to bully or belittle others. (I want to single out Scott Alexander in particular here, who is a nicer person than I am and an increasingly amazing writer on these topics, and may deserve part of the credit for making the culture of *Less Wrong* a healthy one.)

To be able to look backwards and say that you've "failed" implies that you had goals. So what was it that I was trying to do?

There is a certain valuable way of thinking, which is not yet taught in schools, in this present day. This certain way of thinking is not taught systematically at all. It is just absorbed by people who grow up reading books like *Surely You're Joking, Mr. Feynman* or who have an unusually great teacher in high school.

Most famously, this certain way of thinking has to do with science, and with the experimental method. The part of science where you go out and look at the universe instead of just making things up. The part where you say "Oops" and give up on a bad theory when the experiments don't support it.

But this certain way of thinking extends beyond that. It is deeper and more universal than a pair of goggles you put on when you enter a laboratory and take off when you leave. It applies to daily life, though this part is subtler and more difficult. But if you can't say "Oops" and give up when it looks like something isn't working, you have no choice but to keep shooting yourself in the foot. You have to keep reloading the shotgun and you have to keep pulling the trigger. You know people like this. And somewhere, someplace in your life you'd rather not think about, you *are* people like this. It would be nice if there was a certain way of thinking that could help us stop doing that.

In spite of how large my mistakes were, those two years of blog posting appeared to help a surprising number of people a surprising amount. It didn't work reliably, but it worked sometimes.

In modern society so little is taught of the skills of rational belief and decision-making, so little of the mathematics and sciences underlying them . . . that it turns out that just reading through a massive brain-dump full of problems in philosophy and science can, yes, be surprisingly good for you. Walking through all of that, from a dozen different angles, can sometimes convey a glimpse of the central rhythm.

Because it is all, in the end, one thing. I talked about big important distant problems and neglected immediate life, but the laws governing them aren't actually different. There are huge gaps in which parts I focused on, and I picked all the wrong examples; but it is all in the end one thing. I am proud to look back and say that, even after all the mistakes I made, and all the other times I said "Oops" . . .

Even five years later, it still appears to me that this is better than nothing.

—Eliezer Yudkowsky, February 2015

Contents

D Mysterious Answers

Introduction
by Rob Bensinger

Imagine reaching into an urn that contains seventy white balls and thirty red ones, and plucking out ten mystery balls.

Perhaps three of the ten balls will be red, and you'll correctly guess how many red balls total were in the urn. Or perhaps you'll happen to grab four red balls, or some other number. Then you'll probably get the total number wrong.

This random error is the cost of incomplete knowledge, and as errors go, it's not so bad. Your estimates won't be incorrect *on average*, and the more you learn, the smaller your error will tend to be.

On the other hand, suppose that the white balls are heavier, and sink to the bottom of the urn. Then your sample may be unrepresentative *in a consistent direction*.

That kind of error is called "statistical bias." When your method of learning about the world is biased, learning more may not help. Acquiring more data can even consistently *worsen* a biased prediction.

If you're used to holding knowledge and inquiry in high esteem, this is a scary prospect. If we want to be sure that learning more will help us, rather than making us worse off than we were before, we need to discover and correct for biases in our data.

The idea of *cognitive bias* in psychology works in an analogous way. A cognitive bias is a systematic error in *how we think*, as opposed to a random error or one that's merely caused by our ignorance. Whereas statistical bias skews a sample so that it less closely resembles a larger population, cognitive biases skew our thinking so that it less accurately tracks the truth (or less reliably serves our other goals).

Maybe you have an optimism bias, and you find out that the red balls can be used to treat a rare tropical disease besetting your brother, and you end up overestimating how many red balls the urn contains because you *wish* the balls were mostly red.

Like statistical biases, cognitive biases can distort our view of reality, they can't always be fixed by just gathering more data, and their effects can add up over time. But when the miscalibrated measuring instrument you're trying to fix is *you*, debiasing is a unique challenge.

Still, this is an obvious place to start. For if you can't trust your brain, how can you trust anything else?

Noticing Bias

Imagine meeting someone for the first time, and knowing nothing about them except that they're shy.

Question: Is it more likely that this person is a librarian, or a salesperson?

Most people answer "librarian." Which is a mistake: shy salespeople are much more common than shy librarians, because salespeople in general are much more common than librarians—seventy-five times as common, in the United States.[1]

This is *base rate neglect*: grounding one's judgments in how well sets of characteristics feel like they fit together, and neglecting how common each characteristic is in the population at large.[2] Another example of a cognitive bias is the *sunk cost fallacy*—people's tendency to feel committed to things they've spent resources on in the past, when they should be cutting their losses and moving on.

---

[1] Weiten, *Psychology: Themes and Variations, Briefer Version, Eighth Edition,* 2010.
[2] Heuer, *Psychology of Intelligence Analysis,* 1999.

Introduction

Knowing about these biases, unfortunately, doesn't make you immune to them. It doesn't even mean you'll be able to notice them in action.

In a study of *bias blindness*, experimental subjects predicted that they would have a harder time neutrally evaluating the quality of paintings if they knew the paintings were by famous artists. And indeed, these subjects exhibited the very bias they had predicted when the experimenters later tested their prediction. When asked *afterward*, however, the very same subjects claimed that their assessments of the paintings had been objective and unaffected by the bias.[3]

Even when we correctly identify others' biases, we exhibit a *bias blind spot* when it comes to our own flaws.[4] Failing to detect any "biased-feeling thoughts" when we introspect, we draw the conclusion that we must just be less biased than everyone else.[5]

Yet it *is* possible to recognize and overcome biases. It's just not trivial. It's known that subjects can reduce base rate neglect, for example, by thinking of probabilities as frequencies of objects or events.

The approach to debiasing in this book is to communicate a systematic understanding of *why good reasoning works*, and of how the brain falls short of it. To the extent this volume does its job, its approach can be compared to the one described in Serfas (2010), who notes that "years of financially related work experience" didn't affect people's susceptibility to the sunk cost bias, whereas "the number of accounting courses attended" did help.

> As a consequence, it might be necessary to distinguish between experience and expertise, with expertise meaning "the development of a schematic principle that involves conceptual understanding of the problem," which in turn enables the decision maker to recognize particular biases. However, using expertise

---

3 Hansen et al., "People Claim Objectivity After Knowingly Using Biased Strategies," 2014.

4 Pronin, Lin, and Ross, "The Bias Blind Spot: Perceptions of Bias in Self versus Others," 2002.

5 Ehrlinger, Gilovich, and Ross, "Peering Into the Bias Blind Spot: People's Assessments of Bias in Themselves and Others," 2005.

as countermeasure requires more than just being familiar with the situational content or being an expert in a particular domain. It requires that one fully understand the underlying rationale of the respective bias, is able to spot it in the particular setting, and also has the appropriate tools at hand to counteract the bias.[6]

The goal of this book is to lay the groundwork for creating rationality "expertise." That means acquiring a deep understanding of the structure of a very general problem: human bias, self-deception, and the thousand paths by which sophisticated thought can defeat itself.

A Word About This Text

Map and Territory began its life as a series of essays by decision theorist Eliezer Yudkowsky, published between 2006 and 2009 on the economics blog *Overcoming Bias* and its spin-off community blog *Less Wrong*. Thematically linked essays were grouped together in "sequences," and thematically linked sequences were grouped into books. *Map and Territory* is the first of six such books, with the series as a whole going by the name *Rationality: From AI to Zombies*.[7]

In style, this series run the gamut from "lively textbook" to "compendium of vignettes" to "riotous manifesto," and the content is correspondingly varied. The resultant rationality primer is frequently personal and irreverent—drawing, for example, from Yudkowsky's experiences with his Orthodox Jewish mother (a psychiatrist) and father (a physicist), and from conversations on chat rooms and mailing lists. Readers who are familiar with Yudkowsky from *Harry Potter and the Methods of Rationality*, his

---

[6]Serfas, *Cognitive Biases in the Capital Investment Context: Theoretical Considerations and Empirical Experiments on Violations of Normative Rationality*, 2010.

[7]The first edition of *Rationality: From AI to Zombies* was released as a single sprawling ebook, before the series was edited and split up into separate volumes. The full book can also be found on http://lesswrong.com/rationality.

Introduction

science-oriented take-off of J.K. Rowling's *Harry Potter* books, will recognize the same iconoclasm, and many of the same themes.

The philosopher Alfred Korzybski once wrote: "A map *is not* the territory it represents, but, if correct, it has a *similar structure* to the territory, which accounts for its usefulness." And what can be said of maps here, as Korzybski noted, can also be said of beliefs, and assertions, and words.

"The map is not the territory." This deceptively simple claim is the organizing idea behind this book, and behind the four sequences of essays collected here: **Predictably Wrong**, which concerns the systematic ways our beliefs fail to map the real world; **Fake Beliefs**, on what makes a belief a "map" in the first place; **Noticing Confusion**, on how this world-mapping thing our brains do actually works; and **Mysterious Answers**, which collides these points together. The book then concludes with "The Simple Truth," a stand-alone dialogue on the idea of truth itself.

Humans aren't rational; but, as behavioral economist Dan Ariely notes, we're *predictably* irrational. There are patterns to how we screw up. And there are patterns to how we behave when we *don't* screw up. Both admit of fuller understanding, and with it, the hope of leaning on that understanding to build a better future for ourselves.

Acknowledgments

I am stupendously grateful to Nate Soares, Elizabeth Morningstar, Paul Crowley, Brienne Yudkowsky, Adam Freese, Helen Toner, and dozens of volunteers for proofreading portions of this book.

Special and sincere thanks to Alex Vermeer, who steered the original version of this book to completion; to Tsvi Benson-Tilsen, who combed through *Map and Territory* and the other volumes of *Rationality: From AI to Zombies* to ensure their readability and consistency; and to Chana Messinger, whose edits have helped make the text a clearer and more graceful whole.

Part A

Predictably Wrong

Scope Insensitivity

Once upon a time, three groups of subjects were asked how much they would pay to save 2,000 / 20,000 / 200,000 migrating birds from drowning in uncovered oil ponds. The groups respectively answered $80, $78, and $88.[1] This is *scope insensitivity* or *scope neglect*: the number of birds saved—the *scope* of the altruistic action—had little effect on willingness to pay.

Similar experiments showed that Toronto residents would pay little more to clean up all polluted lakes in Ontario than polluted lakes in a particular region of Ontario, or that residents of four western US states would pay only 28% more to protect all 57 wilderness areas in those states than to protect a single area.[2] People visualize "a single exhausted bird, its feathers soaked in black oil, unable to escape."[3] This image, or *prototype*, calls forth some level of emotional arousal that is primarily responsible for willingness-to-pay—and the image is the same in all cases. As for scope, it gets tossed out the window—no human can visualize 2,000 birds at once, let alone 200,000. The usual finding is that *exponential* increases in scope create *linear* increases in willingness-to-pay—perhaps corresponding to the linear time for our eyes to glaze over the zeroes; this small amount of affect is added, not multiplied, with the prototype affect. This hypothesis is known as "valuation by prototype."

An alternative hypothesis is "purchase of moral satisfaction." People spend enough money to create a *warm glow* in themselves, a sense of having

---

[1] Desvousges et al., *Measuring Nonuse Damages Using Contingent Valuation*, 2010.

[2] Kahneman, "Comments by Professor Daniel Kahneman," 1986; McFadden and Leonard, "Issues in the Contingent Valuation of Environmental Goods," 1993.

[3] Kahneman, Ritov, and Schkade, "Economic Preferences or Attitude Expressions?," 1999.

done their duty. The level of spending needed to purchase a warm glow depends on personality and financial situation, but it certainly has nothing to do with the number of birds.

We are insensitive to scope even when human lives are at stake: Increasing the alleged risk of chlorinated drinking water from 0.004 to 2.43 annual deaths per 1,000—a factor of 600—increased willingness-to-pay from $3.78 to $15.23.[4] Baron and Greene found no effect from varying lives saved by a factor of 10.[5]

A paper entitled "Insensitivity to the value of human life: A study of psychophysical numbing" collected evidence that our perception of human deaths follows Weber's Law—obeys a logarithmic scale where the "just noticeable difference" is a constant fraction of the whole. A proposed health program to save the lives of Rwandan refugees garnered far higher support when it promised to save 4,500 lives in a camp of 11,000 refugees, rather than 4,500 in a camp of 250,000. A potential disease cure had to promise to save far more lives in order to be judged worthy of funding, if the disease was originally stated to have killed 290,000 rather than 160,000 or 15,000 people per year.[6]

The moral: If you want to be an effective altruist, you have to think it through with the part of your brain that processes those unexciting inky zeroes on paper, not just the part that gets real worked up about that poor struggling oil-soaked bird.

---

[4]Carson and Mitchell, "Sequencing and Nesting in Contingent Valuation Surveys," 1995.

[5]Baron and Greene, "Determinants of Insensitivity to Quantity in Valuation of Public Goods," 1996.

[6]Fetherstonhaugh et al., "Insensitivity to the Value of Human Life," 1997.

The Martial Art of Rationality

I often use the metaphor that rationality is the martial art of mind. You don't need huge, bulging muscles to learn martial arts—there's a tendency toward more athletic people being more likely to learn martial arts, but that may be a matter of *enjoyment* as much as anything else. If you have a hand, with tendons and muscles in the appropriate places, then you can learn to make a fist.

Similarly, if you have a brain, with cortical and subcortical areas in the appropriate places, you might be able to learn to use it properly. If you're a fast learner, you might learn faster—but the art of rationality isn't about that; it's about training brain machinery we all have in common. And where there are systematic errors human brains tend to make—like an insensitivity to scope—rationality is about fixing those mistakes, or finding work-arounds.

Alas, our minds respond less readily to our will than our hands. Our ability to control our muscles is evolutionarily ancient; our ability to reason about our own reasoning processes is a much more recent innovation. We shouldn't be surprised, then, that muscles are easier to use than brains. But it is not wise to neglect the latter training because it is more difficult. It is not by bigger muscles that the human species rose to prominence upon Earth.

If you live in an urban area, you probably don't need to walk very far to find a martial arts dojo. Why aren't there dojos that teach rationality?

One reason, perhaps, is that it's harder to verify skill. To rise a level in Tae Kwon Do, you might need to break a board of a certain width. If you succeed, all the onlookers can see and applaud. If you fail, your teacher can watch how you shape a fist, and check if you shape it correctly. If not, the teacher holds out a hand and makes a fist correctly, so that you can observe how to do so.

Within martial arts schools, techniques of muscle have been refined and elaborated over generations. Techniques of rationality are harder to pass on, even to the most willing student.

Very recently—in just the last few decades—the human species has acquired a great deal of new knowledge about human rationality. The most salient example would be the heuristics and biases program in experimental psychology. There is also the Bayesian systematization of probability theory and statistics; evolutionary psychology; social psychology. Experimental investigations of empirical human psychology; and theoretical probability theory to interpret what our experiments tell us; and evolutionary theory to explain the conclusions. These fields give us new focusing lenses through which to view the landscape of our own minds. With their aid, we may be able to see more clearly the muscles of our brains, the fingers of thought as they move. We have a shared voc abulary in which to describe problems and solutions. Humanity may finally be ready to synthesize the martial art of mind: to refine, share, systematize, and pass on techniques of personal rationality.

Such understanding as I have of rationality, I acquired in the course of wrestling with the challenge of artificial general intelligence (an endeavor which, to actually succeed, would require sufficient mastery of rationality to build a complete working rationalist out of toothpicks and rubber bands). In most ways the AI problem is enormously more demanding than the personal art of rationality, but in some ways it is actually easier. In the martial art of mind, we need to acquire the realtime procedural skill of pulling the right levers at the right time on a large, pre-existing thinking machine whose innards are not end-user-modifiable. Some of the machinery is optimized for evolutionary selection pressures that run directly counter to our declared goals in using it. Deliberately we decide that we want to seek only the truth; but our brains have hardwired support for rationalizing falsehoods. We can try to compensate for what we choose to regard as flaws of the machinery; but we can't actually rewire the neural circuitry. Nor may martial artists plate titanium over their bones—not today, at any rate.

Trying to synthesize a personal art of rationality, using the science of rationality, may prove awkward: One imagines trying to invent a martial art using an abstract theory of physics, game theory, and human anatomy.

But humans aren't reflectively blind. We do have a native instinct for introspection. The inner eye isn't sightless, though it sees blurrily, with systematic distortions. We need, then, to *apply* the science to our intuitions, to use the abstract knowledge to *correct* our mental movements and *augment* our metacognitive skills.

We aren't writing a computer program to make a string puppet execute martial arts forms; it is our own mental limbs that we must move. Therefore we must connect theory to practice. We must come to see what the science means, for ourselves, for our daily inner life.

3

Availability

The *availability heuristic* is judging the frequency or probability of an event by the ease with which examples of the event come to mind.

A famous 1978 study by Lichtenstein, Slovic, Fischhoff, Layman, and Combs, "Judged Frequency of Lethal Events," studied errors in quantifying the severity of risks, or judging which of two dangers occurred more frequently. Subjects thought that accidents caused about as many deaths as disease; thought that homicide was a more frequent cause of death than suicide. Actually, diseases cause about sixteen times as many deaths as accidents, and suicide is twice as frequent as homicide.

An obvious hypothesis to account for these skewed beliefs is that murders are more likely to be talked about than suicides—thus, someone is more likely to recall hearing about a murder than hearing about a suicide. Accidents are more dramatic than diseases—perhaps this makes people more likely to remember, or more likely to recall, an accident. In 1979, a followup study by Combs and Slovic showed that the skewed probability judgments correlated strongly (0.85 and 0.89) with skewed reporting frequencies in two newspapers. This doesn't disentangle whether murders are more available to memory because they are more reported-on, or whether newspapers report more on murders because murders are more vivid (hence also more remembered). But either way, an availability bias is at work.

Selective reporting is one major source of availability biases. In the ancestral environment, much of what you knew, you experienced yourself; or you heard it directly from a fellow tribe-member who had seen it. There was usually at most one layer of selective reporting between you, and the event itself. With today's Internet, you may see reports that have passed

8

Availability

through the hands of six bloggers on the way to you—six successive filters. Compared to our ancestors, we live in a larger world, in which far more happens, and far less of it reaches us—a much stronger selection effect, which can create much larger availability biases.

In real life, you're unlikely to ever meet Bill Gates. But thanks to selective reporting by the media, you may be tempted to compare your life success to his—and suffer hedonic penalties accordingly. The objective frequency of Bill Gates is 0.00000000015, but you hear about him much more often. Conversely, 19% of the planet lives on less than $1/day, and I doubt that one fifth of the blog posts you read are written by them.

Using availability seems to give rise to an absurdity bias; events that have never happened are not recalled, and hence deemed to have probability zero. When no flooding has recently occurred (and yet the probabilities are still fairly calculable), people refuse to buy flood insurance even when it is heavily subsidized and priced far below an actuarially fair value. Kunreuther et al. suggest underreaction to threats of flooding may arise from "the inability of individuals to conceptualize floods that have never occurred . . . Men on flood plains appear to be very much prisoners of their experience . . . Recently experienced floods appear to set an upward bound to the size of loss with which managers believe they ought to be concerned."[1]

Burton et al. report that when dams and levees are built, they reduce the frequency of floods, and thus apparently create a false sense of security, leading to reduced precautions.[2] While building dams decreases the *frequency* of floods, damage *per flood* is afterward so much greater that average yearly damage *increases*.

The wise would extrapolate from a memory of small hazards to the possibility of large hazards. Instead, past experience of small hazards seems to set a perceived upper bound on risk. A society well-protected against minor hazards takes no action against major risks, building on flood plains

---

[1]Kunreuther, Hogarth, and Meszaros, "Insurer Ambiguity and Market Failure," 1993.

[2]Burton, Kates, and White, *The Environment as Hazard*, 1978.

once the regular minor floods are eliminated. A society subject to regular minor hazards treats those minor hazards as an upper bound on the size of the risks, guarding against regular minor floods but not occasional major floods.

Memory is not always a good guide to probabilities in the past, let alone in the future.

What's a Bias?

The availability heuristic is a cognitive shortcut humans use to reach conclusions; and where this shortcut reliably causes inaccurate conclusions, we can say that an availability bias is at work. Scope insensitivity is another example of a *cognitive bias*.

"Cognitive biases" are those obstacles to truth which are produced, not by the cost of information, nor by limited computing power, but by *the shape of our own mental machinery*. For example, our mental processes might be evolutionarily adapted to specifically believe some things that aren't true, so that we could win political arguments in a tribal context. Or the mental machinery might be adapted not to particularly care whether something is true, such as when we feel the urge to believe what others believe to get along socially. Or the bias may be a side-effect of a useful reasoning heuristic. The availability heuristic is not itself a bias, but it gives rise to them; the machinery uses an algorithm (give things more evidential weight if they come to mind more readily) that does some good cognitive work but also produces systematic errors.

Our brains are doing something wrong, and after a lot of experimentation and/or heavy thinking, someone identifies the problem verbally and concretely; then we call it a "(cognitive) bias." Not to be confused with the colloquial "that person is biased," which just means "that person has a skewed or prejudiced attitude toward something."

In cognitive science, "biases" are distinguished from errors that arise from *cognitive content*, such as learned false beliefs. These we call "mistakes" rather than "biases," and they are much easier to correct, once we've noticed them for ourselves. (Though the source of the mistake, or the source of the source of the mistake, may ultimately be some bias.)

"Biases" are also distinguished from errors stemming from damage to an individual human brain, or from absorbed cultural mores; biases arise from machinery that is humanly universal.

Plato wasn't "biased" because he was ignorant of General Relativity—he had no way to gather that information, his ignorance did not arise from the shape of his mental machinery. But if Plato believed that philosophers would make better kings because he himself was a philosopher—and this belief, in turn, arose because of a universal adaptive political instinct for self-promotion, and not because Plato's daddy told him that everyone has a moral duty to promote their own profession to governorship, or because Plato sniffed too much glue as a kid—then that was a bias, whether Plato was ever warned of it or not.

While I am not averse (as you can see) to discussing definitions, I don't want to suggest that the project of better wielding our own minds rests on a particular choice of terminology. If the term "cognitive bias" turns out to be unhelpful, we should just drop it.

We don't start out with a moral duty to "reduce bias," simply because biases are bad and evil and Just Not Done. This is the sort of thinking someone might end up with if they acquired a deontological duty of "rationality" by social osmosis, which leads to people trying to execute techniques without appreciating the reason for them. (Which is bad and evil and Just Not Done, according to *Surely You're Joking, Mr. Feynman*, which I read as a kid.) A bias is an obstacle to our goal of obtaining truth, and thus *in our way*.

We are here to pursue the great human quest for truth: for we have desperate need of the knowledge, and besides, we're curious. To this end let us strive to overcome whatever obstacles lie in our way, whether we call them "biases" or not.

Burdensome Details

Merely corroborative detail, intended to give artistic verisimilitude to an otherwise bald and unconvincing narrative . . .

—Pooh-Bah, in Gilbert and Sullivan's *The Mikado*

The conjunction fallacy is when humans assign a higher probability to a
proposition of the form "*A* and *B*" than to one of the propositions "*A*" or
"*B*" in isolation, even though it is a theorem that conjunctions are never
likelier than their conjuncts. For example, in one experiment, 68% of the
subjects ranked it more likely that "Reagan will provide federal support for
unwed mothers and cut federal support to local governments" than that
"Reagan will provide federal support for unwed mothers."[1]

A long series of cleverly designed experiments, which weeded out alternative hypotheses and nailed down the standard interpretation, confirmed
that conjunction fallacy occurs because we "substitute judgment of representativeness for judgment of probability."[2] By adding extra details, you
can make an outcome seem *more* characteristic of the process that generates it. You can make it sound more plausible that Reagan will support
unwed mothers, by *adding* the claim that Reagan will *also* cut support to
local governments. The implausibility of one claim is compensated by the
plausibility of the other; they "average out."

---

[1]Tversky and Kahneman, "Judgments of and by Representativeness," 1982.

[2]See Tversky and Kahneman, "Extensional Versus Intuitive Reasoning," 1983 and Kahneman
and Frederick, "Representativeness Revisited: Attribute Substitution in Intuitive Judgment,"
2002 for more information.

Which is to say: Adding detail can make a scenario SOUND MORE PLAUSIBLE, even though the event necessarily BECOMES LESS PROBABLE.

If so, then, *hypothetically speaking*, we might find futurists spinning unconscionably plausible and detailed future histories, or find people swallowing huge packages of unsupported claims bundled with a few strong-sounding assertions at the center.

If you are presented with the conjunction fallacy in a naked, direct comparison, then you may succeed on that particular problem by consciously correcting yourself. But this is only slapping a band-aid on the problem, not fixing it in general.

In the 1982 experiment where professional forecasters assigned systematically higher probabilities to "Russia invades Poland, followed by suspension of diplomatic relations between the USA and the USSR" than to "Suspension of diplomatic relations between the USA and the USSR," each experimental group was only presented with one proposition.[3] What strategy could these forecasters have followed, as a group, that would have eliminated the conjunction fallacy, when no individual knew directly about the comparison? When no individual even knew that the experiment was *about* the conjunction fallacy? How could they have done better on their probability judgments?

Patching one gotcha as a special case doesn't fix the general problem. The gotcha is the symptom, not the disease.

What could the forecasters have done to avoid the conjunction fallacy, without seeing the direct comparison, or even knowing that anyone was going to test them on the conjunction fallacy? It seems to me, that they would need to notice the word "and." They would need to be wary of it—not just wary, but leap back from it. Even without knowing that researchers were afterward going to test them on the conjunction fallacy particularly. They would need to notice the conjunction of *two entire details*, and be *shocked* by the audacity of anyone asking them to endorse such an insanely

---

[3]Tversky and Kahneman, "Extensional Versus Intuitive Reasoning," 1983.

complicated prediction. And they would need to penalize the probability *substantially*—a factor of four, at least, according to the experimental details.

It might also have helped the forecasters to think about possible reasons why the US and Soviet Union would suspend diplomatic relations. The scenario is not "The US and Soviet Union suddenly suspend diplomatic relations for no reason," but "The US and Soviet Union suspend diplomatic relations for any reason."

And the subjects who rated "Reagan will provide federal support for unwed mothers and cut federal support to local governments"? Again, they would need to be shocked by the word "and." Moreover, they would need to *add* absurdities—where the absurdity is the log probability, so you can add it—rather than averaging them. They would need to think, "Reagan might or might not cut support to local governments (1 bit), but it seems very unlikely that he will support unwed mothers (4 bits). *Total* absurdity: 5 bits." Or maybe, "Reagan won't support unwed mothers. One strike and it's out. The other proposition just makes it even worse."

Similarly, consider Tversky and Kahneman's (1983) experiment based around a six-sided die with four green faces and two red faces.[4] The subjects had to bet on the sequence (1) RGRRR, (2) GRGRRR, or (3) GRRRRR appearing anywhere in twenty rolls of the dice. Sixty-five percent of the subjects chose GRGRRR, which is strictly dominated by RGRRR, since any sequence containing GRGRRR also pays off for RGRRR. How could the subjects have done better? By noticing the inclusion? Perhaps; but that is only a band-aid, it does not fix the fundamental problem. By explicitly calculating the probabilities? That would certainly fix the fundamental problem, but you can't always calculate an exact probability.

The subjects lost heuristically by thinking: "Aha! Sequence 2 has the highest proportion of green to red! I should bet on Sequence 2!" To win heuristically, the subjects would need to think: "Aha! Sequence 1 is *short*! I should go with Sequence 1!"

---

[4] Tversky and Kahneman, "Extensional Versus Intuitive Reasoning," 1983.

They would need to feel a stronger *emotional impact* from Occam's Razor—feel *every* added detail as a burden, even a single extra roll of the dice.

Once upon a time, I was speaking to someone who had been mesmerized by an incautious futurist (one who adds on lots of details that sound neat). I was trying to explain why I was not likewise mesmerized by these amazing, incredible theories. So I explained about the conjunction fallacy, specifically the "suspending relations ± invading Poland" experiment. And he said, "Okay, but what does this have to do with—" And I said, "It is more probable that universes replicate *for any reason,* than that they replicate *via black holes because advanced civilizations manufacture black holes because universes evolve to make them do it.*" And he said, "Oh."

Until then, he had not felt these extra details as extra burdens. Instead they were corroborative detail, lending verisimilitude to the narrative. Someone presents you with a package of strange ideas, *one* of which is that universes replicate. Then they present support *for the assertion that universes replicate.* But this is not support for the package, though it is all told as one story.

You have to disentangle the details. You have to hold up every one independently, and ask, "How do we know *this* detail?" Someone sketches out a picture of humanity's descent into nanotechnological warfare, where China refuses to abide by an international control agreement, followed by an arms race . . . Wait a minute—how do you know it will be China? Is that a crystal ball in your pocket or are you just happy to be a futurist? Where are all these details coming from? Where did *that specific* detail come from?

For it is written:

> *If you can lighten your burden you must do so.*
> *There is no straw that lacks the power to break your back.*

6

What Do I Mean By "Rationality"?

I mean two things:

1. **Epistemic rationality:** systematically improving the accuracy of your beliefs.

2. **Instrumental rationality:** systematically achieving your values.

The first concept is simple enough. When you open your eyes and look at the room around you, you'll locate your laptop in relation to the table, and you'll locate a bookcase in relation to the wall. If something goes wrong with your eyes, or your brain, then your mental model might say there's a bookcase where no bookcase exists, and when you go over to get a book, you'll be disappointed.

This is what it's like to have a false belief, a map of the world that doesn't correspond to the territory. Epistemic rationality is about building accurate maps instead. This correspondence between belief and reality is commonly called "truth," and I'm happy to call it that.[1]

Instrumental rationality, on the other hand, is about *steering* reality—sending the future where you want it to go. It's the art of choosing actions that lead to outcomes ranked higher in your preferences. I sometimes call this "winning."

So rationality is about forming true beliefs and making decisions that help you win.

(Where truth doesn't mean "certainty," since we can do plenty to increase the *probability* that our beliefs are accurate even though we're uncertain;

---

[1] For a longer discussion of truth, see "The Simple Truth" at the very end of this volume.

and winning doesn't mean "winning at others' expense," since our values include *everything* we care about, including other people.)

When people say "X is rational!" it's usually just a more strident way of saying "I think X is true" or "I think X is good." So why have an additional word for "rational" as well as "true" and "good"?

An analogous argument can be given against using "true." There is no need to say "it is true that snow is white" when you could just say "snow is white." What makes the idea of truth useful is that it allows us to talk about the general features of map-territory correspondence. "True models usually produce better experimental predictions than false models" is a useful generalization, and it's not one you can make without using a concept like "true" or "accurate."

Similarly, "Rational agents make decisions that maximize the probabilistic expectation of a coherent utility function" is the kind of thought that depends on a concept of (instrumental) rationality, whereas "It's rational to eat vegetables" can probably be replaced with "It's useful to eat vegetables" or "It's in your interest to eat vegetables." We need a concept like "rational" in order to note general facts about those ways of thinking that systematically produce truth or value—and the systematic ways in which we fall short of those standards.

As we've observed in the previous essays, experimental psychologists sometimes uncover human reasoning that seems very strange. For example, someone rates the probability "Bill plays jazz" as *less* than the probability "Bill is an accountant who plays jazz." This seems like an odd judgment, since any particular jazz-playing accountant is obviously a jazz player. But to what higher vantage point do we appeal in saying that the judgment is *wrong*?

Experimental psychologists use two gold standards: *probability theory*, and *decision theory*.

Probability theory is the set of laws underlying rational belief. The mathematics of probability applies equally to "figuring out where your bookcase is" and "estimating how many hairs were on Julius Caesar's head," even though our evidence for the claim "Julius Caesar was bald" is likely to be more complicated and indirect than our evidence for the claim "there's a bookcase in my room." It's all the same problem of how to process the evidence and observations to update one's beliefs. Similarly, decision theory is the set of laws underlying rational action, and is equally applicable regardless of what one's goals and available options are.

Let "P(such-and-such)" stand for "the probability that such-and-such happens," and "$P(A,B)$" for "the probability that both A and B happen." Since it is a universal law of probability theory that $P(A) \geq P(A,B)$, the judgment that P(Bill plays jazz) is less than P(Bill plays jazz, Bill is an accountant) is labeled incorrect.

To keep it technical, you would say that this probability judgment is *non-Bayesian*. Beliefs that conform to a coherent probability distribution, and decisions that maximize the probabilistic expectation of a coherent utility function, are called "Bayesian."

I should emphasize that this *isn't* the notion of rationality that's common in popular culture. People may use the same string of sounds, "ra-tio-nal," to refer to "acting like Mr. Spock of *Star Trek*" and "acting like a Bayesian"; but this doesn't mean that acting Spock-like helps one hair with epistemic or instrumental rationality.[2]

All of this does not quite exhaust the problem of what is meant in practice by "rationality," for two major reasons:

First, the Bayesian formalisms in their full form are computationally intractable on most real-world problems. No one can *actually* calculate and obey the math, any more than you can predict the stock market by calculating the movements of quarks.

---

[2] The idea that "rationality" is about strictly privileging verbal reasoning over feelings is a case in point. Bayesian rationality applies to urges, hunches, perceptions, and wordless intuitions, not just to assertions.

I gave the example of opening your eyes, looking around you, and building a mental model of a room containing a bookcase against the wall. The modern idea of rationality is general enough to include your eyes and your brain's visual areas as things-that-map, and to include instincts and emotions in the belief-and-goal calculus.

Predictably Wrong

This is why there is a whole site called "Less Wrong," rather than a single page that simply states the formal axioms and calls it a day. There's a whole further art to finding the truth and accomplishing value *from inside a human mind*: we have to learn our own flaws, overcome our biases, prevent ourselves from self-deceiving, get ourselves into good emotional shape to confront the truth and do what needs doing, et cetera, et cetera.

Second, sometimes the meaning of the math itself is called into question. The exact rules of probability theory are called into question by, e.g., anthropic problems in which the number of observers is uncertain. The exact rules of decision theory are called into question by, e.g., Newcomb-like problems in which other agents may predict your decision before it happens.[3]

In cases where our best formalizations still come up short, we can return to simpler ideas like "truth" and "winning." If you are a scientist just beginning to investigate fire, it might be a lot wiser to point to a campfire and say "Fire is that orangey-bright hot stuff over there," rather than saying "I define fire as an alchemical transmutation of substances which releases phlogiston." You certainly shouldn't ignore something just because you can't define it. I can't quote the equations of General Relativity from memory, but nonetheless if I walk off a cliff, I'll fall. And we can say the same of cognitive biases and other obstacles to truth—they won't hit any less hard if it turns out we can't define compactly what "irrationality" is.

In cases like these, it is futile to try to settle the problem by coming up with some new definition of the word "rational" and saying, "Therefore my preferred answer, *by definition*, is what is meant by the word 'rational.'" This simply raises the question of why anyone should pay attention to your definition. I'm not interested in probability theory because it is the holy word handed down from Laplace. I'm interested in Bayesian-style belief-updating (with Occam priors) because I expect that this style of thinking

---

[3]For an informal statement of Newcomb's Problem, see Holt, "Thinking Inside the Boxes," 2002, http://www.slate.com/articles/arts/egghead/2002/02/thinkinginside_the_boxes.single.html.

gets us systematically closer to, you know, *accuracy*, the map that reflects the territory.

And then there are questions of how to think that seem not quite answered by either probability theory or decision theory—like the question of how to feel about the truth once you have it. Here, again, trying to define "rationality" a particular way doesn't support an answer, but merely presumes one.

I am not here to argue the meaning of a word, not even if that word is "rationality." The point of attaching sequences of letters to particular concepts is to let two people *communicate*—to help transport thoughts from one mind to another. You cannot change reality, or prove the thought, by manipulating which meanings go with which words.

So if you understand what concept I am *generally getting at* with this word "rationality," and with the sub-terms "epistemic rationality" and "instrumental rationality," we *have communicated*: we have accomplished everything there is to accomplish by talking about how to define "rationality." What's left to discuss is not *what meaning* to attach to the syllables "ra-tio-na-li-ty"; what's left to discuss is *what is a good way to think*.

If you say, "It's (epistemically) rational for me to believe X, but the truth is Y," then you are probably using the word "rational" to mean something other than what I have in mind. (E.g., "rationality" should be *consistent under reflection*—"rationally" looking at the evidence, and "rationally" considering how your mind processes the evidence, shouldn't lead to two different conclusions.)

Similarly, if you find yourself saying, "The (instrumentally) rational thing for me to do is X, but the right thing for me to do is Y," then you are almost certainly using some other meaning for the word "rational" or the word "right." I use the term "rationality" *normatively*, to pick out desirable patterns of thought.

In this case—or in any other case where people disagree about word meanings—you should substitute more specific language in place of "rational": "The self-benefiting thing to do is to run away, but I hope I would at

21

least try to drag the child off the railroad tracks," or "Causal decision theory as usually formulated says you should two-box on Newcomb's Problem, but I'd rather have a million dollars."

In fact, I recommend reading back through this essay, replacing every instance of "rational" with "foozal," and seeing if that changes the connotations of what I'm saying any. If so, I say: strive not for rationality, but for foozality.

The word "rational" has potential pitfalls, but there are plenty of *non*-borderline cases where "rational" works fine to communicate what I'm getting at. Likewise "irrational." In these cases I'm not afraid to use it.

Yet one should be careful not to *overuse* that word. One receives no points merely for pronouncing it loudly. If you speak overmuch of the Way, you will not attain it.

7

Planning Fallacy

The Denver International Airport opened 16 months late, at a cost overrun of $2 billion.[1]

The Eurofighter Typhoon, a joint defense project of several European countries, was delivered 54 months late at a cost of $19 billion instead of $7 billion.

The Sydney Opera House may be the most legendary construction overrun of all time, originally estimated to be completed in 1963 for $7 million, and finally completed in 1973 for $102 million.[2]

Are these isolated disasters brought to our attention by selective availability? Are they symptoms of bureaucracy or government incentive failures? Yes, very probably. But there's also a corresponding cognitive bias, replicated in experiments with individual planners.

Buehler et al. asked their students for estimates of when they (the students) thought they would complete their personal academic projects.[3] Specifically, the researchers asked for estimated times by which the students thought it was 50%, 75%, and 99% probable their personal projects would be done. Would you care to guess how many students finished on or before their estimated 50%, 75%, and 99% probability levels?

- 13% of subjects finished their project by the time they had assigned a 50% probability level;

---

[1] I've also seen $3.1 billion asserted.
[2] Buehler, Griffin, and Ross, "Exploring the 'Planning Fallacy,'" 1994.
[3] Buehler, Griffin, and Ross, "It's About Time," 1995.

- 19% finished by the time assigned a 75% probability level;

- and only 45% (less than half!) finished by the time of their 99% probability level.

As Buehler et al. wrote, "The results for the 99% probability level are especially striking: Even when asked to make a highly conservative forecast, a prediction that they felt virtually certain that they would fulfill, students' confidence in their time estimates far exceeded their accomplishments."[4]

More generally, this phenomenon is known as the "planning fallacy." The planning fallacy is that people think they can plan, ha ha.

A clue to the underlying problem with the planning algorithm was uncovered by Newby-Clark et al., who found that

- Asking subjects for their predictions based on realistic "best guess" scenarios; and

- Asking subjects for their hoped-for "best case" scenarios . . .

. . . produced *indistinguishable* results.[5]

When people are asked for a "realistic" scenario, they envision everything going exactly as planned, with no *unexpected* delays or *unforeseen* catastrophes—the same vision as their "best case."

Reality, it turns out, usually delivers results somewhat worse than the "worst case."

Unlike most cognitive biases, we know a good debiasing heuristic for the planning fallacy. It won't work for messes on the scale of the Denver International Airport, but it'll work for a lot of personal planning, and even some small-scale organizational stuff. Just use an "outside view" instead of an "inside view."

---

[4]Buehler, Griffin, and Ross, "Inside the Planning Fallacy," 2002.

[5]Newby-Clark et al., "People Focus on Optimistic Scenarios and Disregard Pessimistic Scenarios While Predicting Task Completion Times," 2000.

People tend to generate their predictions by thinking about the particular, unique features of the task at hand, and constructing a scenario for how they intend to complete the task—which is just what we usually think of as *planning*.

When you want to get something done, you have to plan out where, when, how; figure out how much time and how much resource is required; visualize the steps from beginning to successful conclusion. All this is the "inside view," and it doesn't take into account unexpected delays and unforeseen catastrophes. As we saw before, asking people to visualize the "worst case" still isn't enough to counteract their optimism—they don't visualize enough Murphyness.

The outside view is when you deliberately *avoid* thinking about the special, unique features of this project, and just ask how long it took to finish *broadly* similar projects in the past. This is counterintuitive, since the inside view has so much more detail—there's a temptation to think that a carefully tailored prediction, taking into account all available data, will give better results.

But experiment has shown that the more detailed subjects' visualization, the more optimistic (and less accurate) they become. Buehler et al. asked an experimental group of subjects to describe highly specific plans for their Christmas shopping—where, when, and how.[6] On average, this group expected to finish shopping more than a week before Christmas. Another group was simply asked when they expected to finish their Christmas shopping, with an average response of four days. Both groups finished an average of three days before Christmas.

Likewise, Buehler et al., reporting on a cross-cultural study, found that Japanese students expected to finish their essays ten days before deadline. They actually finished one day before deadline. Asked when they had previously completed similar tasks, they responded, "one day before deadline." This is the power of the outside view over the inside view.

---

[6] Buehler, Griffin, and Ross, "Inside the Planning Fallacy," 2002.

A similar finding is that experienced outsiders, who know less of the details, but who have relevant memory to draw upon, are often much less optimistic and much more accurate than the actual planners and implementers.

So there is a fairly reliable way to fix the planning fallacy, if you're doing something *broadly* similar to a reference class of previous projects. Just ask how long similar projects have taken in the past, without considering *any* of the special properties of this project. Better yet, ask an experienced outsider how long similar projects have taken.

You'll get back an answer that sounds hideously long, and clearly reflects no understanding of the special reasons why this particular task will take less time. This answer is true. Deal with it.

8

Why Truth?

The goal of instrumental rationality mostly speaks for itself. Some commenters have wondered, on the other hand, why rationalists care about truth. Which invites a few different answers, depending on who you ask; and these different answers have differing characters, which can shape the search for truth in different ways.

You might hold the view that pursuing truth is inherently noble, important, and worthwhile. In which case your priorities will be determined by your ideals about which truths are most important, or about when truth-seeking is most virtuous.

This motivation tends to have a moral character to it. If you think it your duty to look behind the curtain, you are a lot more likely to believe that someone *else* should look behind the curtain too, or castigate them if they deliberately close their eyes.

I tend to be suspicious of morality as a motivation for rationality, *not* because I reject the moral ideal, but because it invites certain kinds of trouble. It is too easy to acquire, as learned moral duties, modes of thinking that are dreadful missteps in the dance.

Consider Spock, the naive archetype of rationality. Spock's affect is always set to "calm," even when wildly inappropriate. He often gives many significant digits for probabilities that are grossly uncalibrated.[1] Yet this popular image is how many people conceive of the duty to be "rational"—small wonder that they do not embrace it wholeheartedly.

---

[1] E.g., "Captain, if you steer the Enterprise directly into that black hole, our probability of surviving is only 2.234%." Yet nine times out of ten the *Enterprise* is not destroyed. What kind of tragic fool gives four significant digits for a figure that is off by two orders of magnitude?

To make rationality into a moral duty is to give it all the dreadful degrees of freedom of an arbitrary tribal custom. People arrive at the wrong answer, and then indignantly protest that they acted with propriety, rather than learning from their mistake.

What other motives are there?

Well, you might want to accomplish some specific real-world goal, like building an airplane, and therefore you need to know some specific truth about aerodynamics. Or more mundanely, you want chocolate milk, and therefore you want to know whether the local grocery has chocolate milk, so you can choose whether to walk there or somewhere else.

If this is the reason you want truth, then the priority you assign to your questions will reflect the expected utility of their information—how much the possible answers influence your choices, how much your choices matter, and how much you expect to find an answer that changes your choice from its default.

To seek truth merely for its instrumental value may seem impure— should we not desire the truth for its own sake?—but such investigations are extremely important because they create an outside criterion of verification: if your airplane drops out of the sky, or if you get to the store and find no chocolate milk, it's a hint that you did something wrong. You get back feedback on which modes of thinking work, and which don't.

Another possibility: you might care about what's true because, damn it, you're *curious*.

As a reason to seek truth, curiosity has a special and admirable purity. If your motive is curiosity, you will assign priority to questions according to how the questions, themselves, tickle your aesthetic sense. A trickier challenge, with a greater probability of failure, may be worth more effort than a simpler one, just because it's more fun.

Curiosity and morality can both attach an intrinsic value to truth. Yet being curious about what's behind the curtain is a very different state of mind from believing that you have a moral duty to look there. If you're curious, your priorities will be determined by which truths you find most intriguing, not most important or most useful.

Although pure curiosity is a wonderful thing, it may not linger too long on verifying its answers, once the attractive mystery is gone. Curiosity, as a human emotion, has been around since long before the ancient Greeks. But what set humanity firmly on the path of Science was noticing that certain modes of thinking uncovered beliefs that let us *manipulate the world*—truth as an instrument. As far as sheer curiosity goes, spinning campfire tales of gods and heroes satisfied that desire just as well, and no one realized that anything was wrong with that.

At the same time, if we're going to improve our skills of rationality, go beyond the standards of performance set by hunter-gatherers, we'll need deliberate beliefs about how to think—things that look like norms of rationalist "propriety." When we write new mental programs for ourselves, they start out as explicit injunctions, and are only slowly (if ever) trained into the neural circuitry that underlies our core motivations and habits.

Curiosity, pragmatism, and quasi-moral injunctions are all key to the rationalist project. Yet if you were to ask me which of these is most foundational, I would say: "curiosity." I have my principles, and I have my plans, which may well tell me to look behind the curtain. But then, I also just really want to know. What will I see? The world has handed me a puzzle, and a solution feels tantalizingly close.

· 9 ·

Feeling Rational

Since curiosity is an emotion, I suspect that some people will object to treating curiosity as a part of rationality. A popular belief about "rationality" is that rationality opposes all emotion—that all our sadness and all our joy are automatically anti-logical by virtue of being *feelings*. Yet strangely enough, I can't find any theorem of probability theory which proves that I should appear ice-cold and expressionless.

When people think of "emotion" and "rationality" as opposed, I suspect that they are really thinking of System 1 and System 2—fast perceptual judgments versus slow deliberative judgments. System 2's deliberative judgments aren't always true, and System 1's perceptual judgments aren't always false; so it is very important to distinguish that dichotomy from "rationality." Both systems can serve the goal of truth, or defeat it, depending on how they are used.

For my part, I label an emotion as "not rational" if it rests on mistaken beliefs, or rather, on mistake-producing epistemic conduct. "If the iron approaches your face, and you believe it is hot, and it is cool, the Way opposes your fear. If the iron approaches your face, and you believe it is cool, and it is hot, the Way opposes your calm." Conversely, an emotion that is evoked by correct beliefs or truth-conducive thinking is a "rational emotion"; and this has the advantage of letting us regard calm as an emotional state, rather than a privileged default.

So is rationality orthogonal to feeling? No; our emotions arise from our models of reality. If I believe that my dead brother has been discovered alive, I will be happy; if I wake up and realize it was a dream, I will be sad. P. C. Hodgell said: "That which can be destroyed by the truth should be."

Feeling Rational

My dreaming self's happiness was opposed by truth. My sadness on waking is rational; there is no truth which destroys it.

Rationality begins by asking how-the-world-is, but spreads virally to any other thought which depends on how we think the world is. Your beliefs about "how-the-world-is" can concern anything you think is out there in reality, anything that either does or does not exist, any member of the class "things that can make other things happen." If you believe that there is a goblin in your closet that ties your shoes' laces together, then this is a belief about how-the-world-is. Your shoes are real—you can pick them up. If there's something out there that can reach out and tie your shoelaces together, it must be real too, part of the vast web of causes and effects we call the "universe."

Feeling angry at the goblin who tied your shoelaces involves a state of mind that is not *just* about how-the-world-is. Suppose that, as a Buddhist or a lobotomy patient or just a very phlegmatic person, finding your shoelaces tied together didn't make you angry. This wouldn't affect what you expected to see in the world—you'd still expect to open up your closet and find your shoelaces tied together. Your anger or calm shouldn't affect your best guess here, because what happens in your closet does not depend on your emotional state of mind; though it may take some effort to think that clearly.

But the angry feeling is tangled up with a state of mind that *is* about how-the-world-is; you become angry *because* you think the goblin tied your shoelaces. The criterion of rationality spreads virally, from the initial question of whether or not a goblin tied your shoelaces, to the resulting anger.

Becoming more rational—arriving at better estimates of how-the-world-is—can diminish feelings *or intensify them*. Sometimes we run away from strong feelings by denying the facts, by flinching away from the view of the world that gave rise to the powerful emotion. If so, then as you study the skills of rationality and train yourself not to deny facts, your feelings will become stronger.

Predictably Wrong

In my early days I was never quite certain whether it was *all right* to feel things strongly—whether it was allowed, whether it was proper. I do not think this confusion arose only from my youthful misunderstanding of rationality. I have observed similar troubles in people who do not even aspire to be rationalists; when they are happy, they wonder if they are really allowed to be happy, and when they are sad, they are never quite sure whether to run away from the emotion or not. Since the days of Socrates at least, and probably long before, the way to appear cultured and sophisticated has been to never let anyone see you care strongly about anything. It's *embarrassing* to feel—it's just not done in polite society. You should see the strange looks I get when people realize how much I care about rationality. It's not the unusual subject, I think, but that they're not used to seeing sane adults who visibly care about *anything*.

But I know, now, that there's nothing wrong with feeling strongly. Ever since I adopted the rule of "That which can be destroyed by the truth should be," I've also come to realize "That which the truth nourishes should thrive." When something good happens, I am happy, and there is no confusion in my mind about whether it is rational for me to be happy. When something terrible happens, I do not flee my sadness by searching for fake consolations and false silver linings. I visualize the past and future of humankind, the tens of billions of deaths over our history, the misery and fear, the search for answers, the trembling hands reaching upward out of so much blood, what we could become someday when we make the stars our cities, all that darkness and all that light—I know that I can never truly understand it, and I haven't the words to say. Despite all my philosophy I am still embarrassed to confess strong emotions, and you're probably uncomfortable hearing them. But I know, now, that it is rational to feel.

The Lens That Sees Its Own Flaws

Light leaves the Sun and strikes your shoelaces and bounces off; some photons enter the pupils of your eyes and strike your retina; the energy of the photons triggers neural impulses; the neural impulses are transmitted to the visual-processing areas of the brain; and there the optical information is processed and reconstructed into a 3D model that is recognized as an untied shoelace; and so you believe that your shoelaces are untied.

Here is the secret of *deliberate rationality*—this whole process is not magic, and you can *understand* it. You can *understand* how you see your shoelaces. You can *think* about which sort of thinking processes will create beliefs which mirror reality, and which thinking processes will not.

Mice can see, but they can't understand seeing. *You* can understand seeing, and because of that, you can do things that mice cannot do. Take a moment to marvel at this, for it is indeed marvelous.

Mice see, but they don't know they have visual cortexes, so they can't correct for optical illusions. A mouse lives in a mental world that includes cats, holes, cheese and mousetraps—but not mouse brains. Their camera does not take pictures of its own lens. But we, as humans, can look at a seemingly bizarre image, and realize that part of what we're seeing is the lens itself. You don't always have to believe your own eyes, but you have to realize that you *have* eyes—you must have distinct mental buckets for the map and the territory, for the senses and reality. Lest you think this a trivial ability, remember how rare it is in the animal kingdom.

The whole idea of Science is, simply, reflective reasoning about a more reliable process for making the contents of your mind mirror the contents of the world. It is the sort of thing mice would never invent. Pondering this business of "performing replicable experiments to falsify theories," we can see *why* it works. Science is not a separate magisterium, far away from real life and the understanding of ordinary mortals. Science is not something that only applies to the inside of laboratories. Science, itself, is an understandable process-in-the-world that correlates brains with reality.

Science *makes sense*, when you think about it. But mice can't think about thinking, which is why they don't have Science. One should not overlook the wonder of this—or the potential power it bestows on us as individuals, not just scientific societies.

Admittedly, understanding the engine of thought may be *a little more complicated* than understanding a steam engine—but it is not a *fundamentally* different task.

Once upon a time, I went to EFNet's #philosophy chatroom to ask, "Do you believe a nuclear war will occur in the next 20 years? If no, why not?" One person who answered the question said he didn't expect a nuclear war for 100 years, because "All of the players involved in decisions regarding nuclear war are not interested right now." "But why extend that out for 100 years?" I asked. "Pure hope," was his reply.

Reflecting on this whole thought process, we can see why the thought of nuclear war makes the person unhappy, and we can see how his brain therefore rejects the belief. But if you imagine a billion worlds—Everett branches, or Tegmark duplicates[1]—this thought process will not systematically correlate optimists to branches in which no nuclear war occurs.[2]

To ask which beliefs make you happy is to turn inward, not outward—it tells you something about yourself, but it is not evidence entangled with

---

[1]Tegmark, "Parallel Universes," 2004, http://arxiv.org/abs/astro-ph/0302131.

[2]Some clever fellow is bound to say, "Ah, but since I have hope, I'll work a little harder at my job, pump up the global economy, and thus help to prevent countries from sliding into the angry and hopeless state where nuclear war is a possibility. So the two events are related after all." At this point, we have to drag in Bayes's Theorem and measure the relationship quantitatively. Your optimistic nature cannot have *that* large an effect on the world; it cannot, of itself, decrease the probability of nuclear war by 20%, or however much your optimistic nature shifted your beliefs. Shifting your beliefs by a large amount, due to an event that only slightly increases your chance of being right, will still mess up your mapping.

the environment. I have nothing against happiness, but it should follow from your picture of the world, rather than tampering with the mental paintbrushes.

If you can see this—if you can see that hope is shifting your *first-order* thoughts by too large a degree—if you can understand your mind as a mapping engine that has flaws—then you can apply a reflective correction. The brain is a flawed lens through which to see reality. This is true of both mouse brains and human brains. But a human brain is a flawed lens that can understand its own flaws—its systematic errors, its biases—and apply second-order corrections to them. This, *in practice,* makes the lens far more powerful. Not perfect, but far more powerful.

Part B

Fake Beliefs

Making Beliefs Pay Rent
(in Anticipated Experiences)

Thus begins the ancient parable:

If a tree falls in a forest and no one hears it, does it make a sound? One says, "Yes it does, for it makes vibrations in the air." Another says, "No it does not, for there is no auditory processing in any brain."

If there's a foundational skill in the martial art of rationality, a mental stance on which all other technique rests, it might be this one: the ability to spot, inside your own head, psychological signs that you have a mental map of something, and signs that you don't.

Suppose that, after a tree falls, the two arguers walk into the forest together. Will one expect to see the tree fallen to the right, and the other expect to see the tree fallen to the left? Suppose that before the tree falls, the two leave a sound recorder next to the tree. Would one, playing back the recorder, expect to hear something different from the other? Suppose they attach an electroencephalograph to any brain in the world; would one expect to see a different trace than the other?

Though the two argue, one saying "No," and the other saying "Yes," they do not anticipate any different experiences. The two think they have different models of the world, but they have no difference with respect to what they expect will *happen to* them; their maps of the world do not diverge in any sensory detail.

It's tempting to try to eliminate this mistake class by insisting that the only legitimate kind of belief is an anticipation of sensory experience. But the world does, in fact, contain much that is not sensed directly. We don't see the atoms underlying the brick, but the atoms are in fact there. There is a floor beneath your feet, but you don't *experience* the floor directly; you see the light *reflected* from the floor, or rather, you see what your retina and visual cortex have processed of that light. To infer the floor from seeing the floor is to step back into the unseen causes of experience. It may seem like a very short and direct step, but it is still a step.

You stand on top of a tall building, next to a grandfather clock with an hour, minute, and ticking second hand. In your hand is a bowling ball, and you drop it off the roof. On which tick of the clock will you hear the crash of the bowling ball hitting the ground?

To answer precisely, you must use beliefs like *Earth's gravity is 9.8 meters per second per second*, and *This building is around 120 meters tall*. These beliefs are not wordless anticipations of a sensory experience; they are verbal-ish, propositional. It probably does not exaggerate much to describe these two beliefs as sentences made out of words. But these two beliefs have an inferential *consequence* that is a direct sensory anticipation—if the clock's second hand is on the 12 numeral when you drop the ball, you anticipate seeing it on the 1 numeral when you hear the crash five seconds later. To anticipate sensory experiences as precisely as possible, we must process beliefs that are not anticipations of sensory experience.

It is a great strength of *Homo sapiens* that we can, better than any other species in the world, learn to model the unseen. It is also one of our great weak points. Humans often believe in things that are not only unseen but unreal.

The same brain that builds a network of inferred causes behind sensory experience can also build a network of causes that is not connected to sensory experience, or poorly connected. Alchemists believed that phlogiston caused fire—we could simplistically model their minds by drawing a little node labeled "Phlogiston," and an arrow from this node to their sensory experience of a crackling campfire—but this belief yielded no advance predictions; the link from phlogiston to experience was always configured after the experience, rather than constraining the experience in advance.

Making Beliefs Pay Rent (in Anticipated Experiences)

Or suppose your English professor teaches you that the famous writer Wulky Wilkinsen is actually a "retropositional author," which you can tell because his books exhibit "alienated resublimation." And perhaps your professor knows all this because their professor told them; but all they're able to say about resublimation is that it's characteristic of retropositional thought, and of retropositionality that it's marked by alienated resublimation. What does this mean you should expect from Wulky Wilkinsen's books?

Nothing. The belief, if you can call it that, doesn't connect to sensory experience at all. But you had better remember the propositional assertions that "Wulky Wilkinsen" has the "retropositionality" attribute and also the "alienated resublimation" attribute, so you can regurgitate them on the upcoming quiz. The two beliefs are connected to each other, though still not connected to any anticipated experience.

We can build up whole networks of beliefs that are connected only to each other—call these "floating" beliefs. It is a uniquely human flaw among animal species, a perversion of *Homo sapiens*'s ability to build more general and flexible belief networks.

The rationalist virtue of *empiricism* consists of constantly asking which experiences our beliefs predict—or better yet, prohibit. Do you believe that phlogiston is the cause of fire? Then what do you expect to see happen, because of that? Do you believe that Wulky Wilkinsen is a retropositional author? Then what do you expect to see because of that? No, not "alienated resublimation"; *what experience will happen to you?* Do you believe that if a tree falls in the forest, and no one hears it, it still makes a sound? Then what experience must therefore befall you?

It is even better to ask: what experience *must not* happen to you? Do you believe that *élan vital* explains the mysterious aliveness of living beings? Then what does this belief *not* allow to happen—what would definitely falsify this belief? A null answer means that your belief does not *constrain* experience; it permits *anything* to happen to you. It floats.

When you argue a seemingly factual question, always keep in mind which difference of anticipation you are arguing about. If you can't find the difference of anticipation, you're probably arguing about labels in your belief network—or even worse, floating beliefs, barnacles on your network. If you don't know what experiences are implied by Wulky Wilkinsen's writing being retropositional, you can go on arguing forever.

Above all, don't ask what to believe—ask what to anticipate. Every question of belief should flow from a question of anticipation, and that question of anticipation should be the center of the inquiry. Every guess of belief should begin by flowing to a specific guess of anticipation, and should continue to pay rent in future anticipations. If a belief turns deadbeat, evict it.

・ 12 ・

A Fable of Science and Politics

In the time of the Roman Empire, civic life was divided between the Blue and Green factions. The Blues and the Greens murdered each other in single combats, in ambushes, in group battles, in riots. Procopius said of the warring factions: "So there grows up in them against their fellow men a hostility which has no cause, and at no time does it cease or disappear, for it gives place neither to the ties of marriage nor of relationship nor of friendship, and the case is the same even though those who differ with respect to these colors be brothers or any other kin."[1] Edward Gibbon wrote: "The support of a faction became necessary to every candidate for civil or ecclesiastical honors."[2]

Who were the Blues and the Greens? They were sports fans—the partisans of the blue and green chariot-racing teams.

Imagine a future society that flees into a vast underground network of caverns and seals the entrances. We shall not specify whether they flee disease, war, or radiation; we shall suppose the first Undergrounders manage to grow food, find water, recycle air, make light, and survive, and that their descendants thrive and eventually form cities. Of the world above, there are only legends written on scraps of paper; and one of these scraps of paper describes the *sky*, a vast open space of air above a great unbounded floor. The sky is cerulean in color, and contains strange floating objects like enormous tufts of white cotton. But the meaning of the word "cerulean"

---

[1] Procopius, *History of the Wars*, 1914.
[2] Gibbon, *The History of the Decline and Fall of the Roman Empire*, 1829.

43

is controversial; some say that it refers to the color known as "blue," and others that it refers to the color known as "green."

In the early days of the underground society, the Blues and Greens contested with open violence; but today, truce prevails—a peace born of a growing sense of pointlessness. Cultural mores have changed; there is a large and prosperous middle class that has grown up with effective law enforcement and become unaccustomed to violence. The schools provide some sense of historical perspective; how long the battle between Blues and Greens continued, how many died, how little changed as a result. Minds have been laid open to the strange new philosophy that people are people, whether they be Blue or Green.

The conflict has not vanished. Society is still divided along Blue and Green lines, and there is a "Blue" and a "Green" position on almost every contemporary issue of political or cultural importance. The Blues advocate taxes on individual incomes, the Greens advocate taxes on merchant sales; the Blues advocate stricter marriage laws, while the Greens wish to make it easier to obtain divorces; the Blues take their support from the heart of city areas, while the more distant farmers and watersellers tend to be Green; the Blues believe that the Earth is a huge spherical rock at the center of the universe, the Greens that it is a huge flat rock circling some other object called a Sun. Not every Blue or every Green citizen takes the "Blue" or "Green" position on every issue, but it would be rare to find a city merchant who believed the sky was blue, and yet advocated an individual tax and freer marriage laws.

The Underground is still polarized; an uneasy peace. A few folk genuinely think that Blues and Greens should be friends, and it is now common for a Green to patronize a Blue shop, or for a Blue to visit a Green tavern. Yet from a truce originally born of exhaustion, there is a quietly growing spirit of tolerance, even friendship.

One day, the Underground is shaken by a minor earthquake. A sightseeing party of six is caught in the tremblor while looking at the ruins of ancient dwellings in the upper caverns. They feel the brief movement of the rock under their feet, and one of the tourists trips and scrapes her knee. The party decides to turn back, fearing further earthquakes. On their way back, one person catches a whiff of something strange in the air, a scent coming from a long-unused passageway. Ignoring the well-meant cautions of fellow travellers, the person borrows a powered lantern and walks into the passageway. The stone corridor wends upward . . . and upward . . . and finally terminates in a hole carved out of the world, a place where all stone ends. Distance, endless distance, stretches away into forever; a gathering space to hold a thousand cities. Unimaginably far above, too bright to look at directly, a searing spark casts light over all visible space, the naked filament of some huge light bulb. In the air, hanging unsupported, are great incomprehensible tufts of white cotton. And the vast glowing ceiling above . . . the *color . . . is . . .*

Now history branches, depending on which member of the sightseeing party decided to follow the corridor to the surface.

Aditya the Blue stood under the blue forever, and slowly smiled. It was not a pleasant smile. There was hatred, and wounded pride; it recalled every argument she'd ever had with a Green, every rivalry, every contested promotion. *"You were right all along,"* the sky whispered down at her, *"and now you can prove it."* For a moment Aditya stood there, absorbing the message, glorying in it, and then she turned back to the stone corridor to tell the world. As Aditya walked, she curled her hand into a clenched fist. "The truce," she said, "is over."

Barron the Green stared uncomprehendingly at the chaos of colors for long seconds. Understanding, when it came, drove a pile-driver punch into the pit of his stomach. Tears started from his eyes. Barron thought of the Massacre of Cathay, where a Blue army had massacred every citizen of a Green town, including children; he thought of the ancient Blue general, Annas Rell,

45

who had declared Greens "a pit of disease; a pestilence to be cleansed"; he thought of the glints of hatred he'd seen in Blue eyes and something inside him cracked. *"How can you be on their side?"* Barron screamed at the sky, and then he began to weep; because he knew, standing under the malevolent blue glare, that the universe had always been a place of evil.

Charles the Blue considered the blue ceiling, taken aback. As a professor in a mixed college, Charles had carefully emphasized that Blue and Green viewpoints were equally valid and deserving of tolerance: The sky was a metaphysical construct, and cerulean a color that could be seen in more than one way. Briefly, Charles wondered whether a Green, standing in this place, might not see a green ceiling above; or if perhaps the ceiling would be green at this time tomorrow; but he couldn't stake the continued survival of civilization on that. This was merely a natural phenomenon of some kind, having nothing to do with moral philosophy or society . . . but one that might be readily misinterpreted, Charles feared. Charles sighed, and turned to go back into the corridor. Tomorrow he would come back alone and block off the passageway.

Daria, once Green, tried to breathe amid the ashes of her world. *I will not flinch,* Daria told herself, *I will not look away.* She had been Green all her life, and now she must be Blue. Her friends, her family, would turn from her. *Speak the truth, even if your voice trembles,* her father had told her; but her father was dead now, and her mother would never understand. Daria stared down the calm blue gaze of the sky, trying to accept it, and finally her breathing quietened. *I was wrong,* she said to herself mournfully; *it's not so complicated, after all.* She would find new friends, and perhaps her family would forgive her . . . or, she wondered with a tinge of hope, rise to this same test, standing underneath this same sky? "The sky is blue," Daria said experimentally, and nothing dire happened to her; but she couldn't bring herself to smile. Daria the Blue exhaled sadly, and went back into the world, wondering what she would say.

Eddin, a Green, looked up at the blue sky and began to laugh cynically. The course of his world's history came clear at last; even he couldn't believe they'd been such fools. "Stupid," Eddin said, "stupid, *stupid*, and all the time it was right here." Hatred, murders, wars, and all along it was just a *thing* somewhere, that someone had written about like they'd write about any other thing. No poetry, no beauty, nothing that any sane person would ever care about, just one pointless thing that had been blown out of all proportion. Eddin leaned against the cave mouth wearily, trying to think of a way to prevent this information from blowing up the world, and wondering if they didn't all deserve it.

Ferris gasped involuntarily, frozen by sheer wonder and delight. Ferris's eyes darted hungrily about, fastening on each sight in turn before moving reluctantly to the next; the blue *sky*, the white *clouds*, the vast unknown *outside*, full of places and things (and people?) that no Undergrounder had ever seen. "Oh, so *that's* what color it is," Ferris said, and went exploring.

13

Belief in Belief

Carl Sagan once told a parable of someone who comes to us and claims: "There is a dragon in my garage." Fascinating! We reply that we wish to see this dragon—let us set out at once for the garage! "But wait," the claimant says to us, "it is an *invisible* dragon."

Now as Sagan points out, this doesn't make the hypothesis unfalsifiable. Perhaps we go to the claimant's garage, and although we see no dragon, we hear heavy breathing from no visible source; footprints mysteriously appear on the ground; and instruments show that something in the garage is consuming oxygen and breathing out carbon dioxide.

But now suppose that we say to the claimant, "Okay, we'll visit the garage and see if we can hear heavy breathing," and the claimant quickly says no, it's an *inaudible* dragon. We propose to measure carbon dioxide in the air, and the claimant says the dragon does not breathe. We propose to toss a bag of flour into the air to see if it outlines an invisible dragon, and the claimant immediately says, "The dragon is permeable to flour."

Carl Sagan used this parable to illustrate the classic moral that poor hypotheses need to do fast footwork to avoid falsification. But I tell this parable to make a different point: The claimant must have an accurate model of the situation *somewhere* in their mind, because they can anticipate, in advance, *exactly which experimental results they'll need to excuse.*

Some philosophers have been much confused by such scenarios, asking, "Does the claimant *really* believe there's a dragon present, or not?" As if the human brain only had enough disk space to represent one belief at a time! Real minds are more tangled than that. There are different types of belief; not all beliefs are direct anticipations. The claimant clearly does not *anticipate* seeing anything unusual upon opening the garage door. Otherwise they wouldn't make advance excuses. It may also be that the claimant's pool of propositional beliefs contains the free-floating statement *There is a dragon in my garage.* It may seem, to a rationalist, that these two beliefs should collide and conflict even though they are of different types. Yet it is a physical fact that you can write "The sky is green!" next to a picture of a blue sky without the paper bursting into flames.

The rationalist virtue of empiricism is supposed to prevent us from making this class of mistake. We're supposed to constantly ask our beliefs which experiences they predict, make them pay rent in anticipation. But the dragon-claimant's problem runs deeper, and cannot be cured with such simple advice. It's not exactly *difficult* to connect belief in a dragon to anticipated experience of the garage. If you believe there's a dragon in your garage, then you can expect to open up the door and see a dragon. If you don't see a dragon, then that means there's no dragon in your garage. This is pretty straightforward. You can even try it with your own garage.

No, this invisibility business is a symptom of something much worse.

Depending on how your childhood went, you may remember a time period when you first began to doubt Santa Claus's existence, but you still believed that you were *supposed* to believe in Santa Claus, so you tried to deny the doubts. As Daniel Dennett observes, where it is difficult to believe a thing, it is often much easier to believe that you *ought* to believe it. What does it mean to believe that the Ultimate Cosmic Sky is both perfectly blue and perfectly green? The statement is confusing; it's not even clear what it would *mean* to believe it—what exactly would *be* believed, if you believed. You can much more easily believe that it is *proper*, that it is *good* and *virtuous* and *beneficial*, to believe that the Ultimate Cosmic Sky is both perfectly blue and perfectly green. Dennett calls this "belief in belief."[1]

And here things become complicated, as human minds are wont to do—I think even Dennett oversimplifies how this psychology works in practice.

---

[1]Dennett, *Breaking the Spell: Religion as a Natural Phenomenon*, 2006.

Fake Beliefs

For one thing, if you believe in belief, you cannot admit to yourself that you merely believe in belief. What's virtuous is to *believe*, not to believe in believing; and so if you only believe in belief, instead of believing, you are not virtuous. Nobody will *admit* to themselves, "I don't believe the Ultimate Cosmic Sky is blue and green, but I believe I ought to believe it"—not unless they are unusually capable of acknowledging their own lack of virtue. People don't believe in belief in belief, they just believe in belief.

(Those who find this confusing may find it helpful to study mathematical logic, which trains one to make very sharp distinctions between the proposition P, a proof of P, and a proof that P is provable. There are similarly sharp distinctions between P, wanting P, believing P, wanting to believe P, and believing that you believe P.)

There are different kinds of belief in belief. You may believe in belief explicitly; you may recite in your deliberate stream of consciousness the verbal sentence "It is virtuous to believe that the Ultimate Cosmic Sky is perfectly blue and perfectly green." (While also believing that you believe this, unless you are unusually capable of acknowledging your own lack of virtue.) But there are also less explicit forms of belief in belief. Maybe the dragon-claimant fears the public ridicule that they imagine will result if they publicly confess they were wrong.[2] Maybe the dragon-claimant flinches away from the prospect of admitting to themselves that there is no dragon, because it conflicts with their self-image as the glorious discoverer of the dragon, who saw in their garage what all others had failed to see.

If all our thoughts were deliberate verbal sentences like philosophers manipulate, the human mind would be a great deal easier for humans to understand. Fleeting mental images, unspoken flinches, desires acted upon without acknowledgement—these account for as much of ourselves as words.

While I disagree with Dennett on some details and complications, I still think that Dennett's notion of *belief in belief* is the key insight necessary to

---

[2] Although, in fact, a rationalist would congratulate them, and others are more likely to ridicule the claimant if they go on claiming there's a dragon in their garage.

understand the dragon-claimant. But we need a wider concept of *belief*, not limited to verbal sentences. "Belief" should include unspoken anticipation-controllers. "Belief in belief" should include unspoken cognitive-behavior-guiders. It is not psychologically realistic to say, "The dragon-claimant does not believe there is a dragon in their garage; they believe it is beneficial to believe there is a dragon in their garage." But it is realistic to say the dragon-claimant *anticipates as if* there is no dragon in their garage, and *makes excuses as if* they believed in the belief.

You can possess an ordinary mental picture of your garage, with no dragons in it, which correctly predicts your experiences on opening the door, and never once think the verbal phrase *There is no dragon in my garage.* I even bet it's happened to you—that when you open your garage door or bedroom door or whatever, and expect to see no dragons, no such verbal phrase runs through your mind.

And to flinch away from giving up your belief in the dragon—or flinch away from giving up your *self-image* as a person who believes in the dragon— it is not necessary to explicitly think *I want to believe there's a dragon in my garage.* It is only necessary to flinch away from the prospect of admitting you don't believe.

If someone believes in their belief in the dragon, and also believes in the dragon, the problem is much less severe. They will be willing to stick their neck out on experimental predictions, and perhaps even agree to give up the belief if the experimental prediction is wrong.[3] But when someone makes up excuses *in advance*, it would seem to require that belief and belief in belief have become unsynchronized.

---

3 Although belief in belief can still interfere with this, if the belief itself is not absolutely confident.

14

Religion's Claim to be Non-Disprovable

The earliest account I know of a scientific experiment is, ironically, the story of Elijah and the priests of Baal.

The people of Israel are wavering between Jehovah and Baal, so Elijah announces that he will conduct an experiment to settle it—quite a novel concept in those days! The priests of Baal will place their bull on an altar, and Elijah will place Jehovah's bull on an altar, but neither will be allowed to start the fire; whichever God is real will call down fire on His sacrifice. The priests of Baal serve as control group for Elijah—the same wooden fuel, the same bull, and the same priests making invocations, but to a false god. Then Elijah pours water on his altar—ruining the experimental symmetry, but this was back in the early days—to signify deliberate acceptance of the burden of proof, like needing a 0.05 significance level. The fire comes down on Elijah's altar, which is the experimental observation. The watching people of Israel shout "The Lord is God!"—peer review.

And then the people haul the 450 priests of Baal down to the river Kishon and slit their throats. This is stern, but necessary. You must firmly discard the falsified hypothesis, and do so swiftly, before it can generate excuses to protect itself. If the priests of Baal are allowed to survive, they will start babbling about how religion is a separate magisterium which can be neither proven nor disproven.

Back in the old days, people actually *believed* their religions instead of just *believing in* them. The biblical archaeologists who went in search of Noah's Ark did not think they were wasting their time; they anticipated they might become famous. Only after failing to find confirming evidence—

and finding disconfirming evidence in its place—did religionists execute what William Bartley called *the retreat to commitment,* "I believe because I believe."

Back in the old days, there was no concept of religion's being a separate magisterium. The Old Testament is a stream-of-consciousness culture dump: history, law, moral parables, and yes, models of how the universe works—like the universe being created in six days (which is a metaphor for the Big Bang), or rabbits chewing their cud. (Which is a metaphor for . . .)

Back in the old days, saying the local religion "could not be proven" would have gotten you burned at the stake. One of the core beliefs of Orthodox Judaism is that God appeared at Mount Sinai and said in a thundering voice, "Yeah, it's all true." From a Bayesian perspective that's some darned unambiguous evidence of a superhumanly powerful entity. (Although it doesn't prove that the entity is God *per se,* or that the entity is benevolent—it could be alien teenagers.) The vast majority of religions in human history—excepting only those invented *extremely* recently—tell stories of events that would constitute completely unmistakable evidence if they'd actually happened. The orthogonality of religion and factual questions is a *recent* and strictly *Western* concept. The people who wrote the original scriptures didn't even know the difference.

The Roman Empire inherited philosophy from the ancient Greeks; imposed law and order within its provinces; kept bureaucratic records; and enforced religious tolerance. The New Testament, created during the time of the Roman Empire, bears some traces of modernity as a result. You couldn't invent a story about God completely obliterating the city of Rome (a la Sodom and Gomorrah), because the Roman historians would call you on it, and you couldn't just stone them.

In contrast, the people who invented the Old Testament stories could make up pretty much anything they liked. Early Egyptologists were genuinely shocked to find no trace whatsoever of Hebrew tribes having ever been in Egypt—they weren't expecting to find a record of the Ten Plagues, but they expected to find *something.* As it turned out, they did find something. They found out that, during the supposed time of the Exodus, Egypt ruled much of Canaan. That's one *huge* historical error, but if there are no libraries, nobody can call you on it.

The Roman Empire did have libraries. Thus, the New Testament doesn't claim big, showy, large-scale geopolitical miracles as the Old Testament routinely did. Instead the New Testament claims smaller miracles which nonetheless fit into the same framework of evidence. A boy falls down and froths at the mouth; the cause is an unclean spirit; an unclean spirit could reasonably be expected to flee from a true prophet, but not to flee from a charlatan; Jesus casts out the unclean spirit; therefore Jesus is a true prophet and not a charlatan. This is perfectly ordinary Bayesian reasoning, if you grant the basic premise that epilepsy is caused by demons (and that the end of an epileptic fit proves the demon fled).

Not only did religion used to make claims about factual and scientific matters, religion used to make claims about *everything*. Religion laid down a code of law—before legislative bodies; religion laid down history—before historians and archaeologists; religion laid down the sexual morals—before Women's Lib; religion described the forms of government—before constitutions; and religion answered scientific questions from biological taxonomy to the formation of stars.[1] The modern concept of religion as purely *ethical* derives from every other area's having been taken over by better institutions. Ethics is what's *left*.

Or rather, people *think* ethics is what's left. Take a culture dump from 2,500 years ago. Over time, humanity will progress immensely, and pieces of the ancient culture dump will become ever more glaringly obsolete. Ethics has not been immune to human progress—for example, we now frown upon such Bible-approved practices as keeping slaves. Why do people *think* that ethics is still fair game?

---

[1] The Old Testament *doesn't* talk about a sense of wonder at the complexity of the universe, perhaps because it was too busy laying down the death penalty for women who wore men's clothing, which was solid and satisfying religious content of that era.

Religion's Claim to be Non-Disprovable

Intrinsically, there's nothing small about the ethical problem with slaughtering thousands of innocent first-born male children to convince an unelected Pharaoh to release slaves who logically could have been teleported out of the country. It should be *more* glaring than the comparatively trivial scientific error of saying that grasshoppers have four legs. And yet, if you say the Earth is flat, people will look at you like you're crazy. But if you say the Bible is your source of ethics, women will not slap you. Most people's concept of rationality is determined by what they think they can get away with; they think they can get away with endorsing Bible ethics; and so it only requires a manageable effort of self-deception for them to overlook the Bible's moral problems. Everyone has agreed not to notice the elephant in the living room, and this state of affairs can sustain itself for a time.

Maybe someday, humanity will advance further, and anyone who endorses the Bible as a source of ethics will be treated the same way as Trent Lott endorsing Strom Thurmond's presidential campaign. And then it will be said that religion's "true core" has always been genealogy or something.

The idea that religion is a separate magisterium that *cannot be proven or disproven* is a Big Lie—a lie which is repeated over and over again, so that people will say it without thinking; yet which is, on critical examination, simply false. It is a wild distortion of how religion happened historically, of how all scriptures present their beliefs, of what children are told to persuade them, and of what the majority of religious people on Earth still believe. You have to admire its sheer brazenness, on a par with *Oceania has always been at war with Eastasia*. The prosecutor whips out the bloody axe, and the defendant, momentarily shocked, thinks quickly and says: "But you can't disprove my innocence by mere evidence—it's a separate magisterium!"

And if that doesn't work, grab a piece of paper and scribble yourself a Get Out of Jail Free card.

* 15 *

Professing and Cheering

I once attended a panel on the topic, "Are science and religion compatible?" One of the women on the panel, a pagan, held forth interminably upon how she believed that the Earth had been created when a giant primordial cow was born into the primordial abyss, who licked a primordial god into existence, whose descendants killed a primordial giant and used its corpse to create the Earth, etc. The tale was long, and detailed, and more absurd than the Earth being supported on the back of a giant turtle. And the speaker clearly knew enough science to know this.

I still find myself struggling for words to describe what I saw as this woman spoke. She spoke with . . . pride? Self-satisfaction? A deliberate flaunting of herself?

The woman went on describing her creation myth for what seemed like forever, but was probably only five minutes. That strange pride/satisfaction/flaunting clearly had something to do with her *knowing* that her beliefs were scientifically outrageous. And it wasn't that she hated science; as a panelist she professed that religion and science were compatible. She even talked about how it was quite understandable that the Vikings talked about a primordial abyss, given the land in which they lived—explained away her own religion!—and yet nonetheless insisted this was what she "believed," said with peculiar satisfaction.

I'm not sure that Daniel Dennett's concept of "belief in belief" stretches to cover this event. It was weirder than that. She didn't recite her creation myth with the fanatical faith of someone who needs to reassure herself. She didn't act like she expected us, the audience, to be convinced—or like she needed our belief to validate her.

Professing and Cheering

Dennett, in addition to introducing the idea of belief in belief, has also suggested that much of what is called "religious belief" should really be studied as "religious profession" instead. Suppose an alien anthropologist studied a group of English students who all seemingly *believed* that Wulky Wilkensen was a retropositional author. The appropriate question may not be "Why do the students all believe this strange belief?" but "Why do they all write this strange sentence on quizzes?" Even if a sentence is essentially meaningless, you can still know when you are supposed to chant the response aloud.

I think Dennett may be slightly too cynical in suggesting that religious profession is *just* saying the belief aloud—most people are honest enough that, if they say a religious statement aloud, they will also feel obligated to say the verbal sentence into their own stream of consciousness.

But even the concept of "religious profession" doesn't seem to cover the pagan woman's claim to believe in the primordial cow. If you had to profess a religious belief to satisfy a priest, or satisfy a co-religionist—heck, to satisfy your own self-image as a religious person—you would have to *pretend* to believe *much more convincingly* than this woman was doing. As she recited her tale of the primordial cow, she wasn't even *trying* to be persuasive on that front—wasn't even trying to convince us that she took her own religion seriously. I think that's the part that so took me aback. I know people who believe they believe ridiculous things, but when they profess them, they'll spend much more effort to convince themselves that they take their beliefs seriously.

It finally occurred to me that this woman wasn't trying to convince us or even convince herself. Her recitation of the creation story wasn't *about* the creation of the world at all. Rather, by launching into a five-minute diatribe about the primordial cow, she was *cheering for paganism*, like holding up a banner at a football game. A banner saying Go Blues isn't a statement of fact, or an attempt to persuade; it doesn't have to be convincing—it's a cheer.

Fake Beliefs

That strange flaunting pride . . . it was like she was marching naked in a gay pride parade.[1] It wasn't just a cheer, like marching, but an outrageous cheer, like marching naked—believing that she couldn't be arrested or criticized, because she was doing it for her pride parade.

That's why it mattered to her that what she was saying was beyond ridiculous. If she'd tried to make it sound more plausible, it would have been like putting on clothes.

---

[1] Of course, there's nothing wrong with *actually* marching naked in pride parades; this isn't something that truth can destroy.

16

Belief as Attire

I have so far distinguished between belief as anticipation-controller, belief in belief, professing, and cheering. Of these, we might call anticipation-controlling beliefs "proper beliefs" and the other forms "improper beliefs." A proper belief can be wrong or irrational, as when someone genuinely anticipates that prayer will cure their sick baby. But the other forms are arguably "not belief at all."

Yet another form of improper belief is belief as group identification—as a way of belonging. Robin Hanson uses the excellent metaphor of wearing unusual clothing, a group uniform like a priest's vestments or a Jewish skullcap, and so I will call this "belief as attire."

In terms of humanly realistic psychology, the Muslims who flew planes into the World Trade Center undoubtedly saw themselves as heroes defending truth, justice, and the Islamic Way from hideous alien monsters a la the movie *Independence Day*. Only a very inexperienced nerd, the sort of nerd who has no idea how non-nerds see the world, would say this out loud in an Alabama bar. It is not an American thing to say. The American thing to say is that the terrorists "hate our freedom" and that flying a plane into a building is a "cowardly act." You cannot say the phrases "heroic self-sacrifice" and "suicide bomber" in the same sentence, even for the sake of accurately describing how the Enemy sees the world. The very *concept* of the courage and altruism of a suicide bomber is Enemy attire—you can tell, because the Enemy talks about it. The cowardice and sociopathy of a suicide bomber is American attire. There are no quote marks you can use to talk about how the Enemy sees the world; it would be like dressing up as a Nazi for Halloween.

Fake Beliefs

Belief-as-attire may help explain how people can be *passionate* about improper beliefs. Mere belief in belief, or religious professing, would have some trouble creating genuine, deep, powerful emotional effects. Or so I suspect; I confess I'm not an expert here. But my impression is this: People who've stopped anticipating-as-if their religion is true, will go to great lengths to *convince* themselves they are passionate, and this desperation can be mistaken for passion. But it's not the same fire they had as a child.

On the other hand, it is very easy for a human being to genuinely, passionately, gut-level belong to a group, to cheer for their favorite sports team.[1] Identifying with a tribe is a very strong emotional force. People will die for it. And once you get people to identify with a tribe, the beliefs which are attire of that tribe will be spoken with the full passion of belonging to that tribe.

---

[1]This is the foundation on which rests the swindle of "Republicans vs. Democrats" and analogous false dilemmas in other countries, but that's a topic for another time.

17

Pretending to be Wise

The hottest place in Hell is reserved for those who in time of crisis remain neutral.

—~~Dante Alighieri, famous hell expert~~
John F. Kennedy, misquoter

Belief is quantitative, and just as it is possible to make overconfident assertions relative to one's anticipations, it is possible to make *under*confident assertions relative to one's anticipations. One can wear the attire of uncertainty, or profess an agnosticism that isn't really there. Here, I'll single out a special case of improper uncertainty: the display of *neutrality* or *suspended judgment* in order to signal maturity, impartiality, or a superior vantage point.

An example would be the case of my parents, who respond to theological questions like "Why does ancient Egypt, which had good records on many other matters, lack any records of Jews having ever been there?" with "Oh, when I was your age, I also used to ask that sort of question, but now I've grown out of it."

Another example would be the principal who, faced with two children who were caught fighting on the playground, sternly says: "It doesn't matter who started the fight, it only matters who ends it." Of course it matters who started the fight. The principal may not have access to good *information* about this critical fact, but if so, the principal should *say* so, not *dismiss the importance* of who threw the first punch. Let a parent try punching the principal, and we'll see how far "It doesn't matter who started it" gets in front of a judge. But to adults it is just *inconvenient* that children fight, and it matters not at all to their *convenience* which child started it. It is only *convenient* that the fight end as rapidly as possible.

A similar dynamic, I believe, governs the occasions in international diplomacy where Great Powers sternly tell smaller groups to stop that fighting *right now*. It doesn't matter to the Great Power who started it—who provoked, or who responded disproportionately to provocation—because the Great Power's ongoing *inconvenience* is only a function of the ongoing conflict. Oh, can't Israel and Hamas just get along?

This I call "pretending to be Wise." Of course there are many ways to try and signal wisdom. But trying to signal wisdom by refusing to make guesses—refusing to sum up evidence—refusing to pass judgment—refusing to take sides—staying above the fray and looking down with a lofty and condescending gaze—which is to say, signaling wisdom by saying and doing nothing—well, that I find particularly pretentious.

Paolo Freire said, "Washing one's hands of the conflict between the powerful and the powerless means to side with the powerful, not to be neutral."[1] A playground is a great place to be a bully, and a terrible place to be a victim, if the teachers don't care *who started it*. And likewise in international politics: A world where the Great Powers refuse to take sides and only demand immediate truces is a great world for aggressors and a terrible place for the aggressed. But, of course, it is a very convenient world in which to be a Great Power or a school principal. So part of this behavior can be chalked up to sheer selfishness on the part of the Wise.

But part of it also has to do with signaling a superior vantage point. After all—what would the *other adults* think of a principal who actually seemed to be *taking sides* in a fight between mere *children*? Why, it would lower the principal's status to a mere *participant in the fray*!

Similarly with the revered elder—who might be a CEO, a prestigious academic, or a founder of a mailing list—whose reputation for fairness depends on their refusal to pass judgment themselves, when others are

---

[1]Freire, *The Politics of Education: Culture, Power, and Liberation*, 1985, 122.

choosing sides. Sides appeal to them for support, but almost always in vain; for the Wise are revered judges on the condition that they almost never actually judge—*then* they would just be another disputant in the fray, no better than any mere arguer.[2]

There *are* cases where it is rational to suspend judgment, where people leap to judgment only because of their biases. As Michael Rooney said:

> The error here is similar to one I see all the time in beginning philosophy students: when confronted with reasons to be skeptics, they instead become relativists. That is, when the rational conclusion is to suspend judgment about an issue, all too many people instead conclude that any judgment is as plausible as any other.

But then how can we avoid the (related but distinct) pseudo-rationalist behavior of signaling your unbiased impartiality by falsely claiming that the current balance of evidence is neutral? "Oh, well, of course you have a lot of passionate Darwinists out there, but I think the evidence we have doesn't really enable us to make a definite endorsement of natural selection over intelligent design."

On this point I'd advise remembering that *neutrality is a definite judgment*. It is not staying *above* anything. It is putting forth the definite and particular position that the balance of evidence in a particular case licenses *only* one summation, which happens to be neutral. This belief, too, must pay rent in anticipated experiences, and it can be wrong; propounding neutrality is just as attackable as propounding any particular side.

Likewise with policy questions. If someone says that both pro-life and pro-choice sides have good points and that they really should try to compromise and respect each other more, they are not taking a position

---

[2]Oddly, judges in the actual legal system can repeatedly hand down real verdicts without *automatically* losing their reputation for impartiality. Maybe because of the understood norm that they *have* to judge, that it's their job. Or maybe because judges don't have to repeatedly rule on issues that have split a tribe on which they depend for their reverence.

above the two standard sides in the abortion debate. They are putting forth a definite judgment, every bit as particular as saying "pro-life!" or "pro-choice!"

It may be useful to initially avoid using issues like abortion or the Israeli-Palestinian conflict for your rationality practice, and so build up skill on less emotionally charged topics. But it's *not* that a rationalist is too mature to talk about politics. It's *not* that a rationalist is above this foolish fray in which only mere political partisans and youthful enthusiasts would stoop to participate.

As Robin Hanson describes it, the ability to have potentially divisive conversations is a limited resource. If you can think of ways to pull the rope sideways, you are justified in expending your limited resources on relatively less common issues where marginal discussion offers relatively higher marginal payoffs.[3]

But then the responsibilities that you deprioritize are a matter of your limited resources. *Not* a matter of floating high above, serene and Wise.

In sum, there's a difference between:

- Passing neutral judgment;

- Declining to invest marginal resources;

- Pretending that either of the above is a mark of deep wisdom, maturity, and a superior vantage point; with the corresponding implication that the original sides occupy lower vantage points that are not importantly different from up there.

---

[3]See Hanson, "Policy Tug-O-War" (http://www.overcomingbias.com/2007/05/policy_tugowar.html) and "Beware Value Talk" (http://www.overcomingbias.com/2009/02/the-cost-of-talking-values.html).

18

Applause Lights

At the Singularity Summit 2007, one of the speakers called for democratic, multinational development of artificial intelligence. So I stepped up to the microphone and asked:

> Suppose that a group of democratic republics form a consortium to develop AI, and there's a lot of politicking during the process—some interest groups have unusually large influence, others get shafted—in other words, the result looks just like the products of modern democracies. Alternatively, suppose a group of rebel nerds develops an AI in their basement, and instructs the AI to poll everyone in the world—dropping cellphones to anyone who doesn't have them—and do whatever the majority says. Which of these do you think is more "democratic," and would you feel safe with either?

I wanted to find out whether he believed in the pragmatic adequacy of the democratic political process, or if he believed in the moral rightness of voting. But the speaker replied:

> The first scenario sounds like an editorial in *Reason* magazine, and the second sounds like a Hollywood movie plot.

Confused, I asked:

> Then what kind of democratic process *did* you have in mind?

The speaker replied:

Something like the Human Genome Project—that was an internationally sponsored research project.

I asked:

How would different interest groups resolve their conflicts in a structure like the Human Genome Project?

And the speaker said:

I don't know.

This exchange puts me in mind of a quote from some dictator or other, who was asked if he had any intentions to move his pet state toward democracy:

We believe we are already within a democratic system. Some factors are still missing, like the expression of the people's will.

The substance of a democracy is the specific mechanism that resolves policy conflicts. If all groups had the same preferred policies, there would be no need for democracy—we would automatically cooperate. The resolution process can be a direct majority vote, or an elected legislature, or even a voter-sensitive behavior of an artificial intelligence, but it has to be *something*. What does it *mean* to call for a "democratic" solution if you don't have a conflict-resolution mechanism in mind?

I think it means that you have said the word "democracy," so the audience is supposed to cheer. It's not so much a propositional statement or belief, as the equivalent of the "Applause" light that tells a studio audience when to clap.

This case is remarkable only in that I mistook the applause light for a policy suggestion, with subsequent embarrassment for all. Most applause lights are much more blatant, and can be detected by a simple reversal test. For example, suppose someone says:

We need to balance the risks and opportunities of AI.

If you reverse this statement, you get:

Applause Lights

We shouldn't balance the risks and opportunities of AI.

Since the reversal sounds *ab*normal, the unreversed statement is probably normal, implying it does not convey new information.

There are plenty of legitimate reasons for uttering a sentence that would be uninformative in isolation. "We need to balance the risks and opportunities of AI" can introduce a discussion topic; it can emphasize the importance of a specific proposal for balancing; it can criticize an unbalanced proposal. Linking to a normal assertion can convey new information to a bounded rationalist—the link itself may not be obvious. But if *no* specifics follow, the sentence is probably an applause light.

I am tempted to give a talk sometime that consists of *nothing but* applause lights, and see how long it takes for the audience to start laughing:

> I am here to propose to you today that we need to balance the risks and opportunities of advanced artificial intelligence. We should avoid the risks and, insofar as it is possible, realize the opportunities. We should not needlessly confront entirely unnecessary dangers. To achieve these goals, we must plan wisely and rationally. We should not act in fear and panic, or give in to technophobia; but neither should we act in blind enthusiasm. We should respect the interests of all parties with a stake in the Singularity. We must try to ensure that the benefits of advanced technologies accrue to as many individuals as possible, rather than being restricted to a few. We must try to avoid, as much as possible, violent conflicts using these technologies; and we must prevent massive destructive capability from falling into the hands of individuals. We should think through these issues before, not after, it is too late to do anything about them . . .

Part C

Noticing Confusion

19

Focus Your Uncertainty

Will bond yields go up, or down, or remain the same? If you're a TV pundit and your job is to explain the outcome after the fact, then there's no reason to worry. No matter *which* of the three possibilities comes true, you'll be able to explain why the outcome perfectly fits your pet market theory. There's no reason to think of these three possibilities as somehow *opposed* to one another, as *exclusive*, because you'll get full marks for punditry no matter which outcome occurs.

But wait! Suppose you're a *novice* TV pundit, and you aren't experienced enough to make up plausible explanations on the spot. You need to prepare remarks in advance for tomorrow's broadcast, and you have limited time to prepare. In this case, it would be helpful to know *which* outcome will actually occur—whether bond yields will go up, down, or remain the same—because then you would only need to prepare *one* set of excuses.

Alas, no one can possibly foresee the future. What are you to do? You certainly can't use "probabilities." We all know from school that "probabilities" are little numbers that appear next to a word problem, and there aren't any little numbers here. Worse, you *feel* uncertain. You don't remember *feeling* uncertain while you were manipulating the little numbers in word problems. *College classes teaching math* are nice clean places, so math can't apply to life situations that aren't nice and clean. You wouldn't want to inappropriately transfer thinking skills from one context to another. Clearly, this is not a matter for "probabilities."

Nonetheless, you only have 100 minutes to prepare your excuses. You can't spend the entire 100 minutes on "up," and also spend all 100 minutes on "down," and also spend all 100 minutes on "same." You've got to prioritize somehow.

If you needed to justify your time expenditure to a review committee, you would have to spend equal time on each possibility. Since there are no little numbers written down, you'd have no documentation to justify spending different amounts of time. You can hear the reviewers now: *And why, Mr. Finkledinger, did you spend exactly 42 minutes on excuse #3? Why not 41 minutes, or 43? Admit it—you're not being objective! You're playing subjective favorites!*

But, you realize with a small flash of relief, there's no review committee to scold you. This is good, because there's a major Federal Reserve announcement tomorrow, and it seems unlikely that bond prices will remain the same. You don't want to spend 33 precious minutes on an excuse you don't anticipate needing.

Your mind keeps drifting to the explanations you use on television, of why each event plausibly fits your market theory. But it rapidly becomes clear that plausibility can't help you here—all three events are plausible. Fittability to your pet market theory doesn't tell you how to divide your time. There's an uncrossable gap between your 100 minutes of time, which are conserved; versus your ability to explain how an outcome fits your theory, which is unlimited.

And yet . . . even in your uncertain state of mind, it seems that you *anticipate* the three events differently; that you *expect* to need some excuses more than others. And—this is the fascinating part—when you think of something that makes it seem *more* likely that bond prices will go up, then you feel *less* likely to need an excuse for bond prices going down or remaining the same.

It even seems like there's a relation between how much you anticipate each of the three outcomes, and how much time you want to spend preparing each excuse. Of course the relation can't actually be quantified. You have 100 minutes to prepare your speech, but there isn't 100 of anything to divide up in this anticipation business. (Although you do work out that, *if* some particular outcome occurs, then your utility function is logarithmic in time spent preparing the excuse.)

Still . . . your mind keeps coming back to the idea that anticipation is limited, unlike excusability, but like time to prepare excuses. Maybe anticipation should be treated as a *conserved resource*, like money. Your first impulse is to try to get more anticipation, but you soon realize that, even if you get more anticipation, you won't have any more time to prepare your excuses. No, your only course is to *allocate* your *limited supply* of anticipation as best you can.

You're pretty sure you weren't taught anything like that in your statistics courses. They didn't tell you what to do when you *felt* so terribly uncertain. They didn't tell you what to do when there were no little numbers handed to you. Why, even if you tried to use numbers, you might end up using any sort of numbers at all—there's no hint what kind of math to use, if you should be using math! Maybe you'd end up using *pairs* of numbers, right and left numbers, which you'd call DS for Dexter-Sinister . . . or who knows what else? (Though you do have only 100 minutes to spend preparing excuses.)

If only there were an art of *focusing your uncertainty*—of *squeezing* as much anticipation as possible into whichever outcome will *actually happen*!

But what could we call an art like that? And what would the rules be like?

20

What Is Evidence?

The sentence "snow is white" is *true* if and only if snow is white.

—Alfred Tarski

To say of what is, that it is, or of what is not, that it is not, is *true*.

—Aristotle, *Metaphysics IV*

Walking along the street, your shoelaces come untied. Shortly thereafter, for some odd reason, you start *believing* your shoelaces are untied. Light leaves the Sun and strikes your shoelaces and bounces off; some photons enter the pupils of your eyes and strike your retina; the energy of the photons triggers neural impulses; the neural impulses are transmitted to the visual-processing areas of the brain; and there the optical information is processed and reconstructed into a 3D model that is recognized as an untied shoelace. There is a sequence of events, a chain of cause and effect, within the world and your brain, by which you end up believing what you believe. The final outcome of the process is a state of *mind* which mirrors the state of your actual *shoelaces*.

What is *evidence?* It is an event entangled, by links of cause and effect, with whatever you want to know about. If the target of your inquiry is your shoelaces, for example, then the light entering your pupils is evidence entangled with your shoelaces. This should not be confused with the technical sense of "entanglement" used in physics—here I'm just talking about "entanglement" in the sense of two things that end up in correlated states because of the links of cause and effect between them.

What Is Evidence?

Not every influence creates the kind of "entanglement" required for evidence. It's no help to have a machine that beeps when you enter winning lottery numbers, if the machine *also* beeps when you enter *losing* lottery numbers. The light reflected from your shoes would not be useful evidence about your shoelaces, if the photons ended up in the same physical state whether your shoelaces were tied or untied.

To say it abstractly: For an event to be *evidence about* a target of inquiry, it has to happen *differently* in a way that's entangled with the *different* possible states of the target. (To say it technically: There has to be Shannon mutual information between the evidential event and the target of inquiry, relative to your current state of uncertainty about both of them.)

Entanglement can be contagious when processed correctly, which is why you need eyes and a brain. If photons reflect off your shoelaces and hit a rock, the rock won't change much. The rock won't reflect the shoelaces in any helpful way; it won't be detectably different depending on whether your shoelaces were tied or untied. This is why rocks are not useful witnesses in court. A photographic film will contract shoelace-entanglement from the incoming photons, so that the photo can itself act as evidence. If your eyes and brain work correctly, *you* will become tangled up with your own shoelaces.

This is why rationalists put such a heavy premium on the paradoxical-seeming claim that a belief is only really worthwhile if you could, in principle, be persuaded to believe otherwise. If your retina ended up in the same state regardless of what light entered it, you would be blind. Some belief systems, in a rather obvious trick to reinforce themselves, say that certain beliefs are only really worthwhile if you believe them *unconditionally*—no matter what you see, no matter what you think. Your brain is supposed to end up in the same state regardless. Hence the phrase, "blind faith." If what you believe doesn't depend on what you see, you've been blinded as effectively as by poking out your eyeballs.

If your eyes and brain work correctly, your beliefs will end up entangled with the facts. *Rational thought produces beliefs which are themselves evidence.*

75

If your tongue speaks truly, your rational beliefs, which are themselves evidence, can act as evidence for someone else. Entanglement can be transmitted through chains of cause and effect—and if you speak, and another hears, that too is cause and effect. When you say "My shoelaces are untied" over a cellphone, you're sharing your entanglement with your shoelaces with a friend.

Therefore rational beliefs are contagious, among honest folk who believe each other to be honest. And it's why a claim that your beliefs are *not* contagious—that you believe for private reasons which are not transmissible—is so suspicious. If your beliefs are entangled with reality, they *should* be contagious among honest folk.

If your model of reality suggests that the outputs of your thought processes should *not* be contagious to others, then your model says that your beliefs are not themselves evidence, meaning they are not entangled with reality. You should apply a reflective correction, and stop believing.

Indeed, if you *feel*, on a *gut* level, what this all *means*, you will *automatically* stop believing. Because "my belief is not entangled with reality" *means* "my belief is not accurate." As soon as you stop believing " 'snow is white' is true," you should (automatically!) stop believing "snow is white," or something is very wrong.

So try to explain why the kind of thought processes you use systematically produce beliefs that mirror reality. Explain why you think you're rational. Why you think that, using thought processes like the ones you use, minds will end up believing "snow is white" if and only if snow is white. If you *don't* believe that the outputs of your thought processes are entangled with reality, why believe the outputs of your thought processes? It's the same thing, or it should be.

21

Scientific Evidence, Legal Evidence, Rational Evidence

Suppose that your good friend, the police commissioner, tells you in strictest confidence that the crime kingpin of your city is Wulky Wilkinsen. As a rationalist, are you licensed to believe this statement? Put it this way: if you go ahead and insult Wulky, I'd call you foolhardy. Since it is prudent to act as if Wulky has a substantially higher-than-default probability of being a crime boss, the police commissioner's statement must have been strong Bayesian evidence.

Our legal system will not imprison Wulky on the basis of the police commissioner's statement. It is not admissible as *legal evidence*. Maybe if you locked up every person accused of being a crime boss by a police commissioner, you'd *initially* catch a lot of crime bosses, and relatively few people the commissioner just didn't like. But unrestrained power attracts corruption like honey attracts flies: over time, you'd catch fewer and fewer real crime bosses (who would go to greater lengths to ensure anonymity), and more and more innocent victims.

This does not mean that the police commissioner's statement is not rational evidence. It still has a lopsided likelihood ratio, and you'd still be a fool to insult Wulky. But on a *social* level, in pursuit of a social goal, we deliberately define "legal evidence" to include only particular kinds of evidence, such as the police commissioner's own observations on the night of April 4th. All legal evidence should ideally be rational evidence, but not the other way around. We impose special, strong, additional standards before we anoint rational evidence as "legal evidence."

Scientific Evidence, Legal Evidence, Rational Evidence

As I write this sentence at 8:33 p.m., Pacific time, on August 18th, 2007, I am wearing white socks. As a rationalist, are you licensed to believe the previous statement? Yes. Could I testify to it in court? Yes. Is it a *scientific* statement? No, because there is no experiment you can perform yourself to verify it. Science is made up of *generalizations* which apply to many particular instances, so that you can run new real-world experiments which test the generalization, and thereby verify for yourself that the generalization is true, without having to trust anyone's authority. Science is the *publicly reproducible* knowledge of humankind.

Like a court system, science as a social process is made up of fallible humans. We want a protected pool of beliefs that are *especially* reliable. And we want social rules that encourage the generation of such knowledge. So we impose special, strong, additional standards before we canonize rational knowledge as "scientific knowledge," adding it to the protected belief pool. Is a rationalist licensed to believe in the historical existence of Alexander the Great? Yes. We have a rough picture of ancient Greece, untrustworthy but better than maximum entropy. But we are dependent on authorities such as Plutarch; we cannot discard Plutarch and verify everything for ourselves. Historical knowledge is not scientific knowledge.

Is a rationalist licensed to believe that the Sun will rise on September 18th, 2007? Yes—not with absolute certainty, but that's the way to bet.[1] Is this statement, as I write this essay on August 18th, 2007, a *scientific* belief?

It may seem perverse to deny the adjective "scientific" to statements like "The Sun will rise on September 18th, 2007." If Science could not make predictions about future events—events which have *not yet* happened—then it would be useless; it could make no prediction in advance of experiment. The prediction that the Sun will rise is, definitely, an *extrapolation* from scientific generalizations. It is based upon models of the Solar System that you could test for yourself by experiment.

---

[1] Pedants: interpret this as the Earth's rotation and orbit remaining roughly constant relative to the Sun.

But imagine that you're constructing an experiment to verify prediction #27, in a new context, of an accepted theory Q. You may not have any concrete reason to suspect the belief is wrong; you just want to test it in a new context. It seems dangerous to say, *before* running the experiment, that there is a "scientific belief" about the result. There is a "conventional prediction" or "theory Q's prediction." But if you already know the "scientific belief" about the result, why bother to run the experiment?

You begin to see, I hope, why I identify Science with *generalizations*, rather than the history of any one experiment. A historical event happens once; generalizations apply over many events. History is not reproducible; scientific generalizations are.

Is my definition of "scientific knowledge" *true*? That is not a well-formed question. The special standards we impose upon science are pragmatic choices. Nowhere upon the stars or the mountains is it written that $p < 0.05$ shall be the standard for scientific publication. Many now argue that 0.05 is too weak, and that it would be *useful* to lower it to 0.01 or 0.001.

Perhaps future generations, acting on the theory that science is the *public, reproducible* knowledge of humankind, will only label as "scientific" papers published in an open-access journal. If you charge for access to the knowledge, is it part of the knowledge of *humankind*? Can we fully trust a result if people must pay to criticize it?

For myself, I think scientific practice would be better served by the dictum that only open, public knowledge counts. But however we choose to define "science," information in a $20,000/year closed-access journal will still count as Bayesian evidence; and so too, the police commissioner's private assurance that Wulky is the kingpin.

22

How Much Evidence Does It Take?

Previously, I defined *evidence* as "an event entangled, by links of cause and effect, with whatever you want to know about," and *entangled* as "happening differently for different possible states of the target." So how much entanglement—how much rational evidence—is required to support a belief?

Let's start with a question simple enough to be mathematical: How hard would you have to entangle yourself with the lottery in order to win? Suppose there are seventy balls, drawn without replacement, and six numbers to match for the win. Then there are 131,115,985 possible winning combinations, hence a randomly selected ticket would have a 1/131,115,985 probability of winning (0.0000007%). To win the lottery, you would need evidence *selective* enough to visibly favor one combination over 131,115,984 alternatives.

Suppose there are some tests you can perform which discriminate, probabilistically, between winning and losing lottery numbers. For example, you can punch a combination into a little black box that always beeps if the combination is the winner, and has only a 1/4 (25%) chance of beeping if the combination is wrong. In Bayesian terms, we would say the *likelihood ratio* is 4 to 1. This means that the box is 4 times as likely to beep when we punch in a correct combination, compared to how likely it is to beep for an incorrect combination.

There are still a whole lot of possible combinations. If you punch in 20 incorrect combinations, the box will beep on 5 of them by sheer chance (on average). If you punch in all 131,115,985 possible combinations, then while the box is certain to beep for the one winning combination, it will also beep for 32,778,996 losing combinations (on average).

So this box doesn't let you win the lottery, but it's better than nothing. If you used the box, your odds of winning would go from 1 in 131,115,985 to 1 in 32,778,997. You've made some progress toward finding your target, the truth, within the huge space of possibilities.

Suppose you can use another black box to test combinations *twice, independently*. Both boxes are certain to beep for the winning ticket. But the chance of a box beeping for a losing combination is 1/4 *independently* for each box; hence the chance of *both* boxes beeping for a losing combination is 1/16. We can say that the *cumulative* evidence, of two independent tests, has a likelihood ratio of 16:1. The number of losing lottery tickets that pass both tests will be (on average) 8,194,749.

Since there are 131,115,985 possible lottery tickets, you might guess that you need evidence whose strength is around 131,115,985 to 1—an event, or series of events, which is 131,115,985 times more likely to happen for a winning combination than a losing combination. Actually, this amount of evidence would only be enough to give you an *even* chance of winning the lottery. Why? Because if you apply a filter of that power to 131 million losing tickets, there will be, on average, one losing ticket that passes the filter. The winning ticket will also pass the filter. So you'll be left with two tickets that passed the filter, only one of them a winner. Fifty percent odds of winning, if you can only buy one ticket.

A better way of viewing the problem: In the beginning, there is 1 winning ticket and 131,115,984 losing tickets, so your odds of winning are 1:131,115,984. If you use a single box, the odds of it beeping are 1 for a winning ticket and 0.25 for a losing ticket. So we multiply 1:131,115,984 by 1:0.25 and get 1:32,778,996. Adding another box of evidence multiplies the odds by 1:0.25 again, so now the odds are 1 winning ticket to 8,194,749 losing tickets.

It is convenient to measure evidence in bits—not like bits on a hard drive, but mathematician's bits, which are conceptually different. Mathematician's bits are the logarithms, base 1/2, of probabilities. For example, if there are four possible outcomes *A*, *B*, *C*, and *D*, whose probabilities are 50%, 25%, 12.5%, and 12.5%, and I tell you the outcome was "*D*," then I have transmitted three bits of information to you, because I informed you of an outcome whose probability was 1/8.

It so happens that 131,115,984 is slightly less than 2 to the 27th power. So 14 boxes or 28 bits of evidence—an event 268,435,456:1 times more likely to happen if the ticket-hypothesis is true than if it is false—would shift the odds from 1:131,115,984 to 268,435,456:131,115,984, which reduces to 2:1. Odds of 2 to 1 mean two chances to win for each chance to lose, so the *probability* of winning with 28 bits of evidence is 2/3. Adding another box, another 2 bits of evidence, would take the odds to 8:1. Adding yet another two boxes would take the chance of winning to 128:1.

So if you want to license a *strong belief* that you will win the lottery—arbitrarily defined as less than a 1% probability of being wrong—34 bits of evidence about the winning combination should do the trick.

In general, the rules for weighing "how much evidence it takes" follow a similar pattern: The larger the *space of possibilities* in which the hypothesis lies, or the more unlikely the hypothesis seems a priori compared to its neighbors, or the more confident you wish to be, the more evidence you need.

You cannot defy the rules; you cannot form accurate beliefs based on inadequate evidence. Let's say you've got 10 boxes lined up in a row, and you start punching combinations into the boxes. You cannot stop on the first combination that gets beeps from all 10 boxes, saying, "But the odds of that happening for a losing combination are a million to one! I'll just ignore those ivory-tower Bayesian rules and stop here." On average, 131 losing tickets will pass such a test for every winner. Considering the space of possibilities and the prior improbability, you jumped to a too-strong conclusion based on insufficient evidence. That's not a pointless bureaucratic regulation; it's math.

Of course, you can still believe based on inadequate evidence, if that is your whim; but you will not be able to believe *accurately*. It is like trying to drive your car without any fuel, because you don't believe in the fuddy-duddy concept that it ought to take fuel to go places. Wouldn't it be so much more *fun*, and so much less expensive, if we just decided to repeal the law that cars need fuel?

Well, you can try. You can even shut your eyes and pretend the car is moving. But *really* arriving at accurate beliefs requires evidence-fuel, and the further you want to go, the more fuel you need.

23

Einstein's Arrogance

In 1919, Sir Arthur Eddington led expeditions to Brazil and to the island of Principe, aiming to observe solar eclipses and thereby test an experimental prediction of Einstein's novel theory of General Relativity. A journalist asked Einstein what he would do if Eddington's observations failed to match his theory. Einstein famously replied: "Then I would feel sorry for the good Lord. The theory is correct."

It seems like a rather foolhardy statement, defying the trope of Traditional Rationality that experiment above all is sovereign. Einstein seems possessed of an arrogance so great that he would refuse to bend his neck and submit to Nature's answer, as scientists must do. Who can *know* that the theory is correct, in advance of experimental test?

Of course, Einstein did turn out to be right. I try to avoid criticizing people when they are right. If they genuinely deserve criticism, I will not need to wait long for an occasion where they are wrong.

And Einstein may not have been quite so foolhardy as he sounded . . .

To assign more than 50% probability to the correct candidate from a pool of 100,000,000 possible hypotheses, you need at least 27 bits of evidence (or thereabouts). You cannot expect to find the correct candidate without tests that are this strong, because lesser tests will yield more than one candidate that passes all the tests. If you try to apply a test that only has a million-to-one chance of a false positive (~20 bits), you'll end up with a hundred candidates. Just *finding* the right answer, within a large space of possibilities, requires a large amount of evidence.

Traditional Rationality emphasizes justification: "If you want to convince me of X, you've got to present me with Y amount of evidence." I myself often slip into this phrasing, whenever I say something like, "To *justify* believing in this proposition, at more than 99% probability, requires 34 bits of evidence." Or, "In order to assign more than 50% probability to your hypothesis, you need 27 bits of evidence." The Traditional phrasing implies that you start out with a hunch, or some private line of reasoning that leads you to a suggested hypothesis, and then you have to gather "evidence" to *confirm* it—to convince the scientific community, or justify saying that you *believe* in your hunch.

But from a Bayesian perspective, you need an amount of evidence roughly equivalent to the complexity of the hypothesis just to locate the hypothesis in theory-space. It's not a question of justifying anything to anyone. If there's a hundred million alternatives, you need at least 27 bits of evidence just to focus your attention uniquely on the correct answer.

This is true even if you call your guess a "hunch" or "intuition." Hunchings and intuitings are real processes in a real brain. If your brain doesn't have at least 10 bits of genuinely entangled valid Bayesian evidence to chew on, your brain cannot single out a correct 10-bit hypothesis for your attention—consciously, subconsciously, whatever. Subconscious processes can't find one out of a million targets using only 19 bits of entanglement any more than conscious processes can. Hunches can be mysterious to the huncher, but they can't violate the laws of physics.

You see where this is going: *At the time of first formulating the hypothesis*—the very first time the equations popped into his head—Einstein must have had, *already in his possession*, sufficient observational evidence to single out the complex equations of General Relativity for his unique attention. Or he couldn't have gotten them *right*.

Now, how likely is it that Einstein would have *exactly* enough observational evidence to raise General Relativity to the level of his attention, but only justify assigning it a 55% probability? Suppose General Relativity is a 29.3-bit hypothesis. How likely is it that Einstein would stumble across *exactly* 29.5 bits of evidence in the course of his physics reading?

Not likely! If Einstein had enough observational evidence to single out the correct equations of General Relativity in the first place, then he probably had enough evidence to be *damn sure* that General Relativity was true.

In fact, since the human brain is not a perfectly efficient processor of information, Einstein probably had *overwhelmingly more evidence* than would, in principle, be required for a perfect Bayesian to assign massive confidence to General Relativity.

"Then I would feel sorry for the good Lord; the theory is correct." It doesn't sound nearly as appalling when you look at it from that perspective. And remember that General Relativity *was* correct, from all that vast space of possibilities.

24

Occam's Razor

The more complex an explanation is, the more evidence you need just to find it in belief-space. (In Traditional Rationality this is often phrased misleadingly, as "The more complex a proposition is, the more evidence is required to argue for it.") How can we measure the complexity of an explanation? How can we determine how much evidence is required?

Occam's Razor is often phrased as "The simplest explanation that fits the facts." Robert Heinlein replied that the simplest explanation is "The lady down the street is a witch; she did it."

One observes that the length of an English sentence is not a good way to measure "complexity." And "fitting" the facts by merely *failing to prohibit* them is insufficient.

Why, exactly, is the length of an English sentence a poor measure of complexity? Because when you speak a sentence aloud, you are using *labels* for concepts that the listener shares—the receiver has already stored the complexity in them. Suppose we abbreviated Heinlein's whole sentence as "Tldtsiawsdi!" so that the entire explanation can be conveyed in one word; better yet, we'll give it a short arbitrary label like "Fnord!" Does this reduce the complexity? No, because you have to tell the listener in advance that "Tldtsiawsdi!" stands for "The lady down the street is a witch; she did it." "Witch," itself, is a label for some extraordinary assertions—just because we all know what it means doesn't mean the concept is simple.

An enormous bolt of electricity comes out of the sky and hits something, and the Norse tribesfolk say, "Maybe a really powerful agent was angry and threw a lightning bolt." The human brain is the most complex artifact in the known universe. If *anger* seems simple, it's because we don't see all the neural circuitry that's implementing the emotion. (Imagine trying to explain why *Saturday Night Live* is funny, to an alien species with no sense of humor. But don't feel superior; you yourself have no sense of fnord.) The complexity of anger, and indeed the complexity of intelligence, was glossed over by the humans who hypothesized Thor the thunder-agent.

To a human, Maxwell's equations take much longer to explain than Thor. Humans don't have a built-in vocabulary for calculus the way we have a built-in vocabulary for anger. You've got to explain your language, and the language behind the language, and the very concept of mathematics, before you can start on electricity.

And yet it seems that there should be some sense in which Maxwell's equations are *simpler* than a human brain, or Thor the thunder-agent.

There is. It's *enormously* easier (as it turns out) to write a computer program that simulates Maxwell's equations, compared to a computer program that simulates an intelligent emotional mind like Thor.

The formalism of Solomonoff induction measures the "complexity of a description" by the length of the shortest computer program which produces that description as an output. To talk about the "shortest computer program" that does something, you need to specify a space of computer programs, which requires a language and interpreter. Solomonoff induction uses Turing machines, or rather, bitstrings that specify Turing machines. What if you don't like Turing machines? Then there's only a constant complexity penalty to design your own universal Turing machine that interprets whatever code you give it in whatever programming language you like. Different inductive formalisms are penalized by a worst-case constant factor relative to each other, corresponding to the size of a universal interpreter for that formalism.

In the better (in my humble opinion) versions of Solomonoff induction, the computer program does not produce a deterministic prediction, but assigns probabilities to strings. For example, we could write a program to explain a fair coin by writing a program that assigns equal probabilities to all 2^N strings of length N. This is Solomonoff induction's approach to *fitting* the observed data. The higher the probability a program assigns to the observed data, the better that program *fits* the data. And probabilities must sum to 1, so for a program to better "fit" one possibility, it must steal probability mass from some other possibility which will then "fit" much more poorly. There is no superfair coin that assigns 100% probability to heads and 100% probability to tails.

How do we trade off the fit to the data, against the complexity of the program? If you ignore complexity penalties, and think *only* about fit, then you will always prefer programs that claim to deterministically predict the data, assign it 100% probability. If the coin shows HTTHHT, then the program that claims that the coin was fixed to show HTTHHT fits the observed data 64 times better than the program which claims the coin is fair. Conversely, if you ignore fit, and consider *only* complexity, then the "fair coin" hypothesis will always seem simpler than any other hypothesis. Even if the coin turns up HTHHTHHHTHHHHTHHHHHT . . .

Indeed, the fair coin *is* simpler and it fits this data exactly as well as it fits any other string of 20 coinflips—no more, no less—but we see another hypothesis, seeming not too complicated, that fits the data much better.

If you let a program store one more binary bit of information, it will be able to cut down a space of possibilities by half, and hence assign twice as much probability to all the points in the remaining space. This suggests that one bit of program complexity should cost *at least* a "factor of two gain" in the fit. If you try to design a computer program that explicitly stores an outcome like HTTHHT, the six bits that you lose in complexity must destroy all plausibility gained by a 64-fold improvement in fit. Otherwise, you will sooner or later decide that all fair coins are fixed.

Unless your program is being smart, and *compressing* the data, it should do no good just to move one bit from the data into the program description.

The way Solomonoff induction works to predict sequences is that you sum up over all allowed computer programs—if every program is allowed, Solomonoff induction becomes uncomputable—with each program having a prior probability of 1/2 to the power of its code length in bits, and each program is further weighted by its fit to all data observed so far. This gives you a weighted mixture of experts that can predict future bits.

The Minimum Message Length formalism is nearly equivalent to Solomonoff induction. You send a string describing a code, and then you send a string describing the data in that code. Whichever explanation leads to the shortest *total* message is the best. If you think of the set of allowable codes as a space of computer programs, and the code description language as a universal machine, then Minimum Message Length is nearly equivalent to Solomonoff induction.[1]

This lets us see clearly the problem with using "The lady down the street is a witch; she did it" to explain the pattern in the sequence 0101010101. If you're sending a message to a friend, trying to describe the sequence you observed, you would have to say: "The lady down the street is a witch; she made the sequence come out 0101010101." Your accusation of witchcraft wouldn't let you *shorten* the rest of the message; you would still have to describe, in full detail, the data which her witchery caused.

Witchcraft may fit our observations in the sense of qualitatively *permitting* them; but this is because witchcraft permits *everything*, like saying "Phlogiston!" So, even after you say "witch," you still have to describe all the observed data in full detail. You have not *compressed the total length of the message describing your observations* by transmitting the message about witchcraft; you have simply added a useless prologue, increasing the total length.

The real sneakiness was concealed in the word "it" of "A witch did it." A witch did *what?*

Of course, thanks to hindsight bias and anchoring and fake explanations and fake causality and positive bias and motivated cognition, it may seem all too obvious that if a woman is a witch, of *course* she would make the coin come up 0101010101. But I'll get to that soon enough. . .

---

[1] Nearly, because it chooses the *shortest* program, rather than summing up over all programs.

25

Your Strength as a Rationalist

The following happened to me in an IRC chatroom, long enough ago that I was still hanging around in IRC chatrooms. Time has fuzzed the memory and my report may be imprecise.

So there I was, in an IRC chatroom, when someone reports that a friend of his needs medical advice. His friend says that he's been having sudden chest pains, so he called an ambulance, and the ambulance showed up, but the paramedics told him it was nothing, and left, and now the chest pains are getting worse. What should his friend do?

I was confused by this story. I remembered reading about homeless people in New York who would call ambulances just to be taken someplace warm, and how the paramedics always had to take them to the emergency room, even on the 27th iteration. Because if they didn't, the ambulance company could be sued for lots and lots of money. Likewise, emergency rooms are legally obligated to treat anyone, regardless of ability to pay.[1] So I didn't quite understand how the described events could have happened. *Anyone* reporting sudden chest pains should have been hauled off by an ambulance instantly.

And this is where I fell down as a rationalist. I remembered several occasions where my doctor would completely fail to panic at the report of symptoms that seemed, to me, very alarming. And the Medical Establishment was always right. Every single time. I had chest pains myself, at one point, and the doctor patiently explained to me that I was describing chest

---

[1] And the hospital absorbs the costs, which are enormous, so hospitals are closing their emergency rooms . . . It makes you wonder what's the point of having economists if we're just going to ignore them.

muscle pain, not a heart attack. So I said into the IRC channel, "Well, if the paramedics told your friend it was nothing, it must *really be* nothing—they'd have hauled him off if there was the tiniest chance of serious trouble."

Thus I managed to explain the story within my existing model, though the fit still felt a little forced . . .

Later on, the fellow comes back into the IRC chatroom and says his friend made the whole thing up. Evidently this was not one of his more reliable friends.

I should have realized, perhaps, that an unknown acquaintance of an acquaintance in an IRC channel might be less reliable than a published journal article. Alas, belief is easier than disbelief; we believe instinctively, but disbelief requires a conscious effort.[2]

So instead, by dint of mighty straining, I forced my model of reality to explain an anomaly that *never actually happened.* And I *knew* how embarrassing this was. I *knew* that the usefulness of a model is not what it can explain, but what it can't. A hypothesis that forbids nothing, permits everything, and thereby fails to constrain anticipation.

Your strength as a rationalist is your ability to be more confused by fiction than by reality. If you are equally good at explaining any outcome, you have zero knowledge.

We are all weak, from time to time; the sad part is that I *could* have been stronger. I had all the information I needed to arrive at the correct answer, I even *noticed* the problem, and then I ignored it. My feeling of confusion was a Clue, and I threw my Clue away.

---

[2] From McCluskey (2007), "Truth Bias": "[P]eople are more likely to correctly judge that a truthful statement is true than that a lie is false. This appears to be a fairly robust result that is not just a function of truth being the correct guess where the evidence is weak—it shows up in controlled experiments where subjects have good reason not to assume truth[.]" http://www.overcomingbias.com/2007/08/truth-bias.html.

And from Gilbert et al. (1993), "You Can't Not Believe Everything You Read": "Can people comprehend assertions without believing them? [...] Three experiments support the hypothesis that comprehension includes an initial belief in the information comprehended."

Noticing Confusion

I should have paid more attention to that sensation of *still feels a little forced*. It's one of the most important feelings a truthseeker can have, a part of your strength as a rationalist. It is a design flaw in human cognition that this sensation manifests as a quiet strain in the back of your mind, instead of a wailing alarm siren and a glowing neon sign reading:

EITHER YOUR MODEL IS FALSE OR THIS STORY IS WRONG.

26

Absence of Evidence *Is*
Evidence of Absence

From Robyn Dawes's *Rational Choice in an Uncertain World*:

> In fact, this post-hoc fitting of evidence to hypothesis was involved in a most grievous chapter in United States history: the internment of Japanese-Americans at the beginning of the Second World War. When California governor Earl Warren testified before a congressional hearing in San Francisco on February 21, 1942, a questioner pointed out that there had been no sabotage or any other type of espionage by the Japanese-Americans up to that time. Warren responded, "I take the view that this lack [of subversive activity] is the most ominous sign in our whole situation. It convinces me more than perhaps any other factor that the sabotage we are to get, the Fifth Column activities are to get, are timed just like Pearl Harbor was timed . . . I believe we are just being lulled into a false sense of security."

Consider Warren's argument from a Bayesian perspective. When we see evidence, hypotheses that assigned a *higher* likelihood to that evidence gain probability, at the expense of hypotheses that assigned a *lower* likelihood to the evidence. This is a phenomenon of *relative* likelihoods and *relative* probabilities. You can assign a high likelihood to the evidence and still lose probability mass to some other hypothesis, if that other hypothesis assigns a likelihood that is even higher.

Warren seems to be arguing that, given that we see no sabotage, this *confirms* that a Fifth Column exists. You could argue that a Fifth Column *might* delay its sabotage. But the likelihood is still higher that the *absence* of a Fifth Column would perform an absence of sabotage.

Let E stand for the observation of sabotage, and $\neg E$ for the observation of no sabotage. The symbol H_1 stands for the hypothesis of a Japanese-American Fifth Column, and H_2 for the hypothesis that no Fifth Column exists. The *conditional probability* $P(E|H)$, or "E given H," is how confidently we'd expect to see the evidence E if we assumed the hypothesis H were true.

Whatever the likelihood that a Fifth Column would do no sabotage, the probability $P(\neg E|H_1)$, it won't be as large as the likelihood that there's no sabotage *given that there's no Fifth Column*, the probability $P(\neg E|H_2)$. So observing a lack of sabotage increases the probability that no Fifth Column exists.

A lack of sabotage doesn't *prove* that no Fifth Column exists. Absence of *proof* is not *proof* of absence. In logic, $(A \Rightarrow B)$, read "A implies B," is not equivalent to $(\neg A \Rightarrow \neg B)$, read "not-$A$ implies not-B."

But in probability theory, absence of *evidence* is always *evidence* of absence. If E is a binary event and $P(H|E) > P(H)$, i.e., seeing E increases the probability of H, then $P(H|\neg E) < P(H)$, i.e., failure to observe E decreases the probability of H. The probability $P(H)$ is a weighted mix of $P(H|E)$ and $P(H|\neg E)$, and necessarily lies between the two.[1]

Under the vast majority of real-life circumstances, a cause may not reliably produce signs of itself, but the absence of the cause is even less likely to produce the signs. The absence of an observation may be strong evidence of absence or very weak evidence of absence, depending on how likely the cause is to produce the observation. The absence of an observation that is only weakly permitted (even if the alternative hypothesis does not allow it at all) is very weak evidence of absence (though it is evidence nonetheless). This is the fallacy of "gaps in the fossil record"—fossils form only rarely; it is

---

[1] If any of this sounds at all confusing, see my discussion of Bayesian updating toward the end of *The Machine in the Ghost*, the third volume of *Rationality: From AI to Zombies*.

futile to trumpet the absence of a weakly permitted observation when many strong positive observations have already been recorded. But if there are *no* positive observations at all, it is time to worry; hence the Fermi Paradox.

Your strength as a rationalist is your ability to be more confused by fiction than by reality; if you are equally good at explaining any outcome you have zero knowledge. The strength of a model is not what it *can* explain, but what it *can't*, for only prohibitions constrain anticipation. If you don't notice when your model makes the evidence unlikely, you might as well have no model, and also you might as well have no evidence; no brain and no eyes.

27

Conservation of Expected Evidence

Friedrich Spee von Langenfeld, a priest who heard the confessions of condemned witches, wrote in 1631 the *Cautio Criminalis* ("prudence in criminal cases"), in which he bitingly described the decision tree for condemning accused witches: If the witch had led an evil and improper life, she was guilty; if she had led a good and proper life, this too was a proof, for witches dissemble and try to appear especially virtuous. After the woman was put in prison: if she was afraid, this proved her guilt; if she was not afraid, this proved her guilt, for witches characteristically pretend innocence and wear a bold front. Or on hearing of a denunciation of witchcraft against her, she might seek flight or remain; if she ran, that proved her guilt; if she remained, the devil had detained her so she could not get away.

Spee acted as confessor to many witches; he was thus in a position to observe *every* branch of the accusation tree, that no matter *what* the accused witch said or did, it was held as proof against her. In any individual case, you would only hear one branch of the dilemma. It is for this reason that scientists write down their experimental predictions in advance.

But *you can't have it both ways*—as a matter of probability theory, not mere fairness. The rule that "absence of evidence *is* evidence of absence" is a special case of a more general law, which I would name Conservation of Expected Evidence: the *expectation* of the posterior probability, after viewing the evidence, must equal the prior probability.

$$P(H) = P(H,E) + P(H,\neg E)$$
$$P(H) = P(H|E) \times P(E) + P(H|\neg E) \times P(\neg E)$$

Conservation of Expected Evidence

Therefore, for every expectation of evidence, there is an equal and opposite expectation of counterevidence.

If you expect a strong probability of seeing weak evidence in one direction, it must be balanced by a weak expectation of seeing strong evidence in the other direction. If you're very confident in your theory, and therefore anticipate seeing an outcome that matches your hypothesis, this can only provide a very small increment to your belief (it is already close to 1); but the unexpected failure of your prediction would (and must) deal your confidence a huge blow. On *average*, you must expect to be *exactly* as confident as when you started out. Equivalently, the mere *expectation* of encountering evidence—before you've actually seen it—should not shift your prior beliefs.

So if you claim that "no sabotage" is evidence *for* the existence of a Japanese-American Fifth Column, you must conversely hold that seeing sabotage would argue *against* a Fifth Column. If you claim that "a good and proper life" is evidence that a woman is a witch, then an evil and improper life must be evidence that she is not a witch. If you argue that God, to test humanity's faith, refuses to reveal His existence, then the miracles described in the Bible must argue against the existence of God.

Doesn't quite sound right, does it? Pay attention to that feeling of *this seems a little forced*, that quiet strain in the back of your mind. It's important.

For a true Bayesian, it is impossible to seek evidence that *confirms* a theory. There is no possible plan you can devise, no clever strategy, no cunning device, by which you can legitimately expect your confidence in a fixed proposition to be higher (on *average*) than before. You can only ever seek evidence to *test* a theory, not to confirm it.

This realization can take quite a load off your mind. You need not worry about how to interpret every possible experimental result to confirm your theory. You needn't bother planning how to make *any* given iota of evidence confirm your theory, because you know that for every expectation of evidence, there is an equal and oppositive expectation of counterevidence. If you try to weaken the counterevidence of a possible "abnormal" observation, you can only do it by weakening the support of a "normal" observation, to a precisely equal and opposite degree. It is a zero-sum game. No matter how you connive, no matter how you argue, no matter how you strategize, you can't possibly expect the resulting game plan to shift your beliefs (on average) in a particular direction.

You might as well sit back and relax while you wait for the evidence to come in.

. . . Human psychology is *so* screwed up.

28

Hindsight Devalues Science

This essay is closely based on an excerpt from Meyers's Exploring Social Psychology; the excerpt is worth reading in its entirety.

Cullen Murphy, editor of *The Atlantic,* said that the social sciences turn up "no ideas or conclusions that can't be found in [any] encyclopedia of quotations . . . Day after day social scientists go out into the world. Day after day they discover that people's behavior is pretty much what you'd expect."

Of course, the "expectation" is all hindsight. (Hindsight bias: Subjects who know the actual answer to a question assign much higher probabilities they "would have" guessed for that answer, compared to subjects who must guess without knowing the answer.)

The historian Arthur Schlesinger, Jr. dismissed scientific studies of World War II soldiers' experiences as "ponderous demonstrations" of common sense. For example:

1. Better educated soldiers suffered more adjustment problems than less educated soldiers. (Intellectuals were less prepared for battle stresses than street-smart people.)

2. Southern soldiers coped better with the hot South Sea Island climate than Northern soldiers. (Southerners are more accustomed to hot weather.)

3. White privates were more eager to be promoted to noncommissioned officers than Black privates. (Years of oppression take a toll on achievement motivation.)

4. Southern Blacks preferred Southern to Northern White officers. (Southern officers were more experienced and skilled in interacting with Blacks.)

5. As long as the fighting continued, soldiers were more eager to return home than after the war ended. (During the fighting, soldiers knew they were in mortal danger.)

How many of these findings do you think you *could have* predicted in advance? Three out of five? Four out of five? Are there any cases where you would have predicted the opposite—where your model takes a hit? Take a moment to think before continuing . . .

. . .

In this demonstration (from Paul Lazarsfeld by way of Meyers), all of the findings above are the *opposite* of what was actually found.[1] How many times did you think your model took a hit? How many times did you admit you would have been wrong? That's how good your model really was. The measure of your strength as a rationalist is your ability to be more confused by fiction than by reality.

Unless, of course, I reversed the results again. What do you think?

Do your thought processes at this point, where you *really don't* know the answer, feel different from the thought processes you used to rationalize either side of the "known" answer?

---

[1] Lazarsfeld, "The American Solidier—An Expository Review," 1949.

Hindsight Devalues Science

Daphna Baratz exposed college students to pairs of supposed findings, one true ("In prosperous times people spend a larger portion of their income than during a recession") and one the truth's opposite.[2] In both sides of the pair, students rated the supposed finding as what they "would have predicted." Perfectly standard hindsight bias.

Which leads people to think they have no need for science, because they "could have predicted" that.

(Just as you would expect, right?)

Hindsight will lead us to systematically undervalue the surprisingness of scientific findings, especially the discoveries we *understand*—the ones that seem real to us, the ones we can retrofit into our models of the world. If you understand neurology or physics and read news in that topic, then you probably underestimate the surprisingness of findings in those fields too. This unfairly devalues the contribution of the researchers; and worse, will prevent you from noticing when you are seeing evidence that doesn't fit what you *really* would have expected.

We need to make a conscious effort to be shocked *enough*.

---

[2] Baratz, *How Justified Is the "Obvious" Reaction?*, 1983.

29

Illusion of Transparency:
Why No One Understands You

In hindsight bias, people who know the outcome of a situation believe the outcome should have been easy to predict in advance. Knowing the outcome, we reinterpret the situation in light of that outcome. Even when warned, we can't de-interpret to empathize with someone who doesn't know what we know.

Closely related is the *illusion of transparency*: We always know what *we* mean by our words, and so we expect others to know it too. Reading our own writing, the intended interpretation falls easily into place, guided by our knowledge of what we really meant. It's hard to empathize with someone who must interpret blindly, guided only by the words.

June recommends a restaurant to Mark; Mark dines there and discovers (a) unimpressive food and mediocre service or (b) delicious food and impeccable service. Then Mark leaves the following message on June's answering machine: "June, I just finished dinner at the restaurant you recommended, and I must say, it was marvelous, just marvelous." Keysar (1994) presented a group of subjects with scenario (a), and 59% thought that Mark's message was sarcastic *and that Jane would perceive the sarcasm.*[1] Among other subjects, told scenario (b), only 3% thought that Jane would perceive Mark's message as sarcastic. Keysar and Barr (2002) seem to indicate that an actual voice message was played back to the subjects.[2] Keysar (1998) showed that if subjects were told that the restaurant was horrible *but that Mark wanted*

---

[1] Keysar, "The Illusory Transparency of Intention," 1994.

[2] Keysar and Barr, "Self-Anchoring in Conversation," 2002.

to conceal his response, they believed June would not perceive sarcasm in the (same) message:[3]

> They were just as likely to predict that she would perceive sarcasm when he attempted to conceal his negative experience as when he had a positive experience and was truly sincere. So participants took Mark's *communicative intention* as transparent. It was as if they assumed that June would perceive whatever intention Mark wanted her to perceive.[4]

"The goose hangs high" is an archaic English idiom that has passed out of use in modern language. Keysar and Bly (1995) told one group of subjects that "the goose hangs high" meant that the future looks good; another group of subjects learned that "the goose hangs high" meant the future looks gloomy.[5] Subjects were then asked which of these two meanings an *uninformed* listener would be more likely to attribute to the idiom. Each group thought that listeners would perceive the meaning presented as "standard."[6]

Keysar and Henly (2002) tested the calibration of speakers: Would speakers underestimate, overestimate, or correctly estimate how often listeners understood them?[7] Speakers were given ambiguous sentences ("The man is chasing a woman on a bicycle.") and disambiguating pictures (a man running after a cycling woman). Speakers were then asked to utter the words in front of addressees, and asked to estimate how many addressees understood the intended meaning. Speakers thought that they were understood in 72% of cases and were actually understood in 61% of cases. When addressees did not understand, speakers thought they did in 46% of cases; when addressees did understand, speakers thought they did not in only 12% of cases.

---

3 Keysar, "Language Users as Problem Solvers," 1998.

4 The wording here is from Keysar and Barr.

5 Keysar and Bly, "Intuitions of the Transparency of Idioms," 1995.

6 Other idioms tested included "come the uncle over someone," "to go by the board," and "to lay out in lavender." Ah, English, such a lovely language.

7 Keysar and Henly, "Speakers' Overestimation of Their Effectiveness," 2002.

Additional subjects who *overheard* the explanation showed no such bias, expecting listeners to understand in only 56% of cases.

As Keysar and Barr note, two days before Germany's attack on Poland, Chamberlain sent a letter intended to make it clear that Britain would fight if any invasion occurred. The letter, phrased in polite diplomatese, was heard by Hitler as conciliatory—and the tanks rolled.

Be not too quick to blame those who misunderstand your perfectly clear sentences, spoken or written. Chances are, your words are more ambiguous than you think.

30

Expecting Short Inferential Distances

Homo sapiens's environment of evolutionary adaptedness (a.k.a. EEA or "ancestral environment") consisted of hunter-gatherer bands of at most 200 people, with no writing. All inherited knowledge was passed down by speech and memory.

In a world like that, all background knowledge is universal knowledge. All information not strictly private is public, period.

In the ancestral environment, you were unlikely to end up more than *one inferential step* away from anyone else. When you discover a new oasis, you don't have to explain to your fellow tribe members what an oasis is, or why it's a good idea to drink water, or how to walk. Only you know where the oasis lies; this is private knowledge. But everyone has the background to understand your description of the oasis, the concepts needed to think about water; this is universal knowledge. When you explain things in an ancestral environment, you almost *never* have to explain your concepts. At most you have to explain *one* new concept, not two or more simultaneously.

In the ancestral environment there were no abstract disciplines with vast bodies of carefully gathered evidence generalized into elegant theories transmitted by written books whose conclusions are *a hundred inferential steps removed* from universally shared background premises.

In the ancestral environment, anyone who says something with no obvious support is a liar or an idiot. You're not likely to think, "Hey, maybe this person has well-supported background knowledge that no one in my band has even heard of," because it was a reliable invariant of the ancestral environment that this didn't happen.

Conversely, if you say something blatantly obvious and the other person doesn't see it, *they're* the idiot, or they're being deliberately obstinate to annoy you.

And to top it off, if someone says something with no obvious support and *expects* you to believe it—acting all indignant when you don't—then they must be *crazy.*

Combined with the illusion of transparency and self-anchoring (the tendency to model other minds as though the were slightly modified versions of oneself), I think this explains a *lot* about the legendary difficulty most scientists have in communicating with a lay audience—or even communicating with scientists from other disciplines. When I observe failures of explanation, I usually see the explainer taking *one* step back, when they need to take two or more steps back. Or listeners assume that things should be visible in one step, when they take two or more steps to explain. Both sides act as if they expect very short inferential distances from universal knowledge to any new knowledge.

A biologist, speaking to a physicist, can justify evolution by saying it is the simplest explanation. But not everyone on Earth has been inculcated with that legendary history of science, from Newton to Einstein, which invests the phrase "simplest explanation" with its awesome import: a Word of Power, spoken at the birth of theories and carved on their tombstones. To someone else, "But it's the simplest explanation!" may sound like an interesting but hardly knockdown argument; it doesn't feel like all that powerful a tool for comprehending office politics or fixing a broken car. Obviously the biologist is infatuated with their own ideas, too arrogant to be open to alternative explanations which sound just as plausible. (If it sounds plausible to me, it should sound plausible to any sane member of my band.)

And from the biologist's perspective, they can understand how evolution might sound a little odd at first—but when someone rejects evolution even after the biologist explains that it's the simplest explanation, well, it's clear that nonscientists are just idiots and there's no point in talking to them.

Expecting Short Inferential Distances

A clear argument has to lay out an inferential *pathway*, starting from what the audience *already knows or accepts*. If you don't recurse far enough, you're just talking to yourself.

If at any point you make a statement without obvious justification in arguments you've previously supported, the audience just thinks you're crazy.

This also happens when you allow yourself to be seen *visibly* attaching greater weight to an argument than is justified in the eyes of the audience *at that time*. For example, talking as if you think "simpler explanation" is a knockdown argument for evolution (which it is), rather than a sorta-interesting idea (which it sounds like to someone who hasn't been raised to revere Occam's Razor).

Oh, and you'd better not drop any hints that *you* think you're working a dozen inferential steps away from what the audience knows, or that *you* think you have special background knowledge not available to them. The audience doesn't know anything about an evolutionary-psychological argument for a cognitive bias to underestimate inferential distances leading to traffic jams in communication. They'll just think you're condescending.

And if you think you can explain the concept of "systematically underestimated inferential distances" briefly, in just a few words, I've got some sad news for you . . .

Part D

Mysterious Answers

31

Fake Explanations

Once upon a time, there was an instructor who taught physics students. One day the instructor called them into the classroom and showed them a wide, square plate of metal, next to a hot radiator. The students each put their hand on the plate and found the side next to the radiator cool, and the distant side warm. And the instructor said, *Why do you think this happens?* Some students guessed convection of air currents, and others guessed strange metals in the plate. They devised many creative explanations, none stooping so low as to say "I don't know" or "This seems impossible."

And the answer was that before the students entered the room, the instructor turned the plate around.[1]

Consider the student who frantically stammers, "Eh, maybe because of the heat conduction and so?" I ask: Is this answer a proper belief? The words are easily enough professed—said in a loud, emphatic voice. But do the words actually control anticipation?

Ponder that innocent little phrase, "because of," which comes before "heat conduction." Ponder some of the *other* things we could put after it. We could say, for example, "Because of phlogiston," or "Because of magic."

"Magic!" you cry. "That's not a *scientific* explanation!" Indeed, the phrases "because of heat conduction" and "because of magic" are readily recognized as belonging to different *literary genres*. "Heat conduction" is something that Spock might say on *Star Trek*, whereas "magic" would be said by Giles in *Buffy the Vampire Slayer*.

---

[1] Verhagen, *Science Jokes*, 2001, http://web.archive.org/web/20060424082937/http://www.nvon.nl/scheik/best/diversen/scijokes/scijokes.txt.

However, as Bayesians, we take no notice of literary genres. For us, the substance of a model is the control it exerts on anticipation. If you say "heat conduction," what experience does that lead you to *anticipate*? Under normal circumstances, it leads you to anticipate that, if you put your hand on the side of the plate near the radiator, that side will feel warmer than the opposite side. If "because of heat conduction" can also explain the radiator-adjacent side feeling *cooler*, then it can explain pretty much *anything*.

And as we all know by this point (I do hope), if you are equally good at explaining any outcome, you have zero knowledge. "Because of heat conduction," used in such fashion, is a disguised hypothesis of maximum entropy. It is anticipation-isomorphic to saying "magic." It feels like an explanation, but it's not.

Suppose that instead of guessing, we measured the heat of the metal plate at various points and various times. Seeing a metal plate next to the radiator, we would ordinarily expect the point temperatures to satisfy an equilibrium of the diffusion equation with respect to the boundary conditions imposed by the environment. You might not know the exact temperature of the first point measured, but after measuring the first points—I'm not physicist enough to know how many would be required—you could take an excellent guess at the rest.

A true master of the art of using numbers to constrain the anticipation of material phenomena—a "physicist"—would take some measurements and say, "This plate was in equilibrium with the environment two and a half minutes ago, turned around, and is now approaching equilibrium again."

The deeper error of the students is not simply that they failed to constrain anticipation. Their deeper error is that they thought they were doing physics. They said the phrase "because of," followed by the sort of words Spock might say on *Star Trek*, and thought they thereby entered the magisterium of science.

Not so. They simply moved their magic from one literary genre to another.

32

Guessing the Teacher's Password

When I was young, I read popular physics books such as Richard Feynman's *QED: The Strange Theory of Light and Matter*. I knew that light was waves, sound was waves, matter was waves. I took pride in my scientific literacy, when I was nine years old.

When I was older, and I began to read the *Feynman Lectures on Physics*, I ran across a gem called "the wave equation." I could follow the equation's derivation, but, looking back, I couldn't see its truth at a glance. So I thought about the wave equation for three days, on and off, until I saw that it was embarrassingly obvious. And when I finally understood, I realized that the whole time I had accepted the honest assurance of physicists that light was waves, sound was waves, matter was waves, I had not had the vaguest idea of what the word "wave" meant to a physicist.

There is an instinctive tendency to think that if a physicist says "light is made of waves," and the teacher says "What is light made of?" and the student says "Waves!", then the student has made a true statement. That's only fair, right? We accept "waves" as a correct answer from the physicist; wouldn't it be unfair to reject it from the student? Surely, the answer "Waves!" is either *true* or *false*, right?

Which is one more bad habit to unlearn from school. Words do not have intrinsic definitions. If I hear the syllables "bea-ver" and think of a large rodent, that is a fact about my own state of mind, not a fact about the syllables "bea-ver." The sequence of syllables "made of waves" (or "because of heat conduction") is not a *hypothesis*; it is a pattern of vibrations traveling through the air, or ink on paper. It can *associate* to a hypothesis in someone's mind, but it is not, of itself, right or wrong. But in school, the teacher hands you a gold star for *saying* "made of waves," which must be the correct answer because the teacher heard a physicist emit the same sound-vibrations. Since verbal behavior (spoken or written) is what gets the gold star, students begin to think that verbal behavior has a truth-value. After all, either light is made of waves, or it isn't, right?

And this leads into an even worse habit. Suppose the teacher asks you why the far side of a metal plate feels warmer than the side next to the radiator. If you say "I don't know," you have *no* chance of getting a gold star—it won't even count as class participation. But, during the current semester, this teacher has used the phrases "because of heat convection," "because of heat conduction," and "because of radiant heat." One of these is probably what the teacher wants. You say, "Eh, maybe because of heat conduction?"

This is not a hypothesis *about* the metal plate. This is not even a proper belief. It is an attempt to *guess the teacher's password.*

Even visualizing the symbols of the diffusion equation (the math governing heat conduction) doesn't mean you've formed a hypothesis *about* the metal plate. This is not school; we are not testing your memory to see if you can write down the diffusion equation. This is Bayescraft; we are scoring your anticipations of experience. If you *use* the diffusion equation, by measuring a few points with a thermometer and then trying to predict what the thermometer will say on the next measurement, then it is definitely connected to experience. Even if the student just visualizes something *flowing,* and therefore holds a match near the cooler side of the plate to try to measure where the heat goes, then this mental image of flowing-ness connects to experience; it controls anticipation.

If you aren't *using* the diffusion equation—putting in numbers and getting out results that control your anticipation of particular experiences— then the connection between map and territory is severed as though by a knife. What remains is not a belief, but a verbal behavior.

In the school system, it's all about verbal behavior, whether written on paper or spoken aloud. Verbal behavior gets you a gold star or a failing grade. Part of unlearning this bad habit is becoming consciously aware of the difference between an explanation and a password.

Does this seem too harsh? When you're faced by a confusing metal plate, can't "heat conduction?" be a first step toward finding the answer? Maybe, but only if you don't fall into the trap of thinking that you are looking for a password. What if there is no teacher to tell you that you failed? Then you may think that "Light is wakalixes" is a good explanation, that "wakalixes" is the correct password. It happened to me when I was nine years old—not because I was stupid, but because this is what happens *by default*. This is how human beings think, unless they are trained *not* to fall into the trap. Humanity stayed stuck in holes like this for thousands of years.

Maybe, if we drill students that *words don't count, only anticipation-controllers*, the student will *not* get stuck on "Heat conduction? No? Maybe heat convection? That's not it either?" Maybe *then*, thinking the phrase "heat conduction" will lead onto a genuinely helpful path, like:

- "Heat conduction?"

- But that's only a phrase—what does it mean?

- The diffusion equation?

- But those are only symbols—how do I apply them?

- What does applying the diffusion equation lead me to anticipate?

- It sure doesn't lead me to anticipate that the side of a metal plate farther away from a radiator would feel warmer.

- I notice that I am confused. Maybe the near side just *feels* cooler, because it's made of more insulative material and transfers less heat to my hand? I'll try measuring the temperature . . .

- Okay, that wasn't it. Can I try to verify whether the diffusion equation holds true of this metal plate, at all? Is heat *flowing* the way it usually does, or is something else going on?

- I could hold a match to the plate and try to measure how heat spreads over time . . .

If we are *not* strict about "Eh, maybe because of heat conduction?" being a fake explanation, the student will very probably get stuck on some wakalixes-password. *This happens by default: it happened to the whole human species for thousands of years.*

Science as Attire

The preview for the *X-Men* movie has a voice-over saying: "In every human being . . . there is the genetic code . . . for mutation." Apparently you can acquire all sorts of neat abilities by mutation. The mutant Storm, for example, has the ability to throw lightning bolts.

I beg you, dear reader, to consider the biological machinery necessary to generate electricity; the biological adaptations necessary to avoid being harmed by electricity; and the cognitive circuitry required for finely tuned control of lightning bolts. If we actually observed any organism acquiring these abilities *in one generation,* as the result of *mutation,* it would outright falsify the neo-Darwinian model of natural selection. It would be worse than finding rabbit fossils in the pre-Cambrian. If evolutionary theory could *actually* stretch to cover Storm, it would be able to explain anything, and we all know what that would imply.

The *X-Men* comics use terms like "evolution," "mutation," and "genetic code," purely to place themselves in what they conceive to be the *literary genre* of science. The part that scares me is wondering how many people, especially in the media, understand science *only* as a literary genre.

I encounter people who very definitely believe in evolution, who sneer at the folly of creationists. And yet they have no idea of what the theory of evolutionary biology permits and prohibits. They'll talk about "the next step in the evolution of humanity," as if natural selection got here by following a plan. Or even worse, they'll talk about something completely outside the domain of evolutionary biology, like an improved design for computer chips, or corporations splitting, or humans uploading themselves into computers, and they'll call *that* "evolution." If evolutionary biology could cover that, it could cover anything.

Probably an actual majority of the people who *believe in* evolution use the phrase "because of evolution" because they want to be part of the scientific in-crowd—belief as scientific attire, like wearing a lab coat. If the scientific in-crowd instead used the phrase "because of intelligent design," they would just as cheerfully use that instead—it would make no difference to their anticipation-controllers. Saying "because of evolution" instead of "because of intelligent design" does not, *for them*, prohibit Storm. Its only purpose, for them, is to identify with a tribe.

I encounter people who are quite willing to entertain the notion of dumber-than-human artificial intelligence, or even mildly smarter-than-human artificial intelligence. Introduce the notion of strongly superhuman artificial intelligence, and they'll suddenly decide it's "pseudoscience." It's not that they think they have a theory of intelligence which lets them calculate a theoretical upper bound on the power of an optimization process. Rather, they associate strongly superhuman AI to the *literary genre* of apocalyptic literature; whereas an AI running a small corporation associates to the literary genre of *Wired* magazine. They aren't speaking from within a model of cognition. They don't realize they *need* a model. They don't realize that science is *about* models. Their devastating critiques consist purely of *comparisons to apocalyptic literature*, rather than, say, known laws which prohibit such an outcome. They understand science *only* as a literary genre, or in-group to belong to. The attire doesn't look to them like a lab coat; this isn't the football team they're cheering for.

Is there any idea in science that you are *proud* of believing, though you do not use the belief professionally? You had best ask yourself which future experiences your belief *prohibits* from happening to you. That is the sum of what you have assimilated and made a true part of yourself. Anything else is probably passwords or attire.

· 34 ·

Fake Causality

Phlogiston was the eighteenth century's answer to the Elemental Fire of the Greek alchemists. Ignite wood, and let it burn. What is the orangey-bright "fire" stuff? Why does the wood transform into ash? To both questions, the eighteenth-century chemists answered, "phlogiston."

. . . and that was it, you see, that was their answer: "Phlogiston."

Phlogiston escaped from burning substances as visible fire. As the phlogiston escaped, the burning substances lost phlogiston and so became ash, the "true material." Flames in enclosed containers went out because the air became saturated with phlogiston, and so could not hold any more. Charcoal left little residue upon burning because it was nearly pure phlogiston.

Of course, one didn't use phlogiston theory to *predict* the outcome of a chemical transformation. You looked at the result first, then you used phlogiston theory to *explain* it. It's not that phlogiston theorists predicted a flame would extinguish in a closed container; rather they lit a flame in a container, watched it go out, and then said, "The air must have become saturated with phlogiston." You couldn't even use phlogiston theory to say what you ought *not* to see; it could explain everything.

This was an earlier age of science. For a long time, no one realized there was a problem. Fake explanations don't *feel* fake. That's what makes them dangerous.

Modern research suggests that humans think about cause and effect using something like the directed acyclic graphs (DAGs) of Bayes nets. Because it rained, the sidewalk is wet; because the sidewalk is wet, it is slippery:

From this we can infer—or, in a Bayes net, rigorously calculate in probabilities—that when the sidewalk is slippery, it probably rained; but if we already know that the sidewalk is wet, learning that the sidewalk is slippery tells us nothing more about whether it rained.

Why is fire hot and bright when it burns?

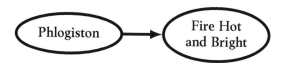

It *feels* like an explanation. It's *represented* using the same cognitive data format. But the human mind does not automatically detect when a cause has an unconstraining arrow to its effect. Worse, thanks to hindsight bias, it may feel like the cause constrains the effect, when it was merely fitted to the effect.

Interestingly, our modern understanding of probabilistic reasoning about causality can describe precisely what the phlogiston theorists were doing wrong. One of the primary inspirations for Bayesian networks was noticing the problem of double-counting evidence if inference resonates between an effect and a cause. For example, let's say that I get a bit of un-reliable information that the sidewalk is wet. This should make me think it's more likely to be raining. But, if it's more likely to be raining, doesn't that make it more likely that the sidewalk is wet? And wouldn't *that* make it more likely that the sidewalk is slippery? But if the sidewalk is slip-pery, it's probably wet; and then I should again raise my probability that it's raining . . .

Judea Pearl uses the metaphor of an algorithm for counting soldiers in a line. Suppose you're in the line, and you see two soldiers next to you, one in front and one in back. That's three soldiers, including you. So you ask the soldier behind you, "How many soldiers do *you* see?" They look around and say, "Three." So that's a total of six soldiers. This, obviously, is *not* how to do it.

A smarter way is to ask the soldier in front of you, "How many soldiers forward of you?" and the soldier in back, "How many soldiers backward of you?" The question "How many soldiers forward?" can be passed on as a message without confusion. If I'm at the front of the line, I pass the message "1 soldier forward," for myself. The person directly in back of me gets the message "1 soldier forward," and passes on the message "2 soldiers forward" to the soldier behind them. At the same time, each soldier is also getting the message "N soldiers backward" from the soldier behind them, and passing it on as "$N + 1$ soldiers backward" to the soldier in front of them. How many soldiers in total? Add the two numbers you receive, plus one for yourself: that is the total number of soldiers in line.

The key idea is that every soldier must *separately* track the two messages, the forward-message and backward-message, and add them together only at the end. You never add any soldiers from the backward-message you receive to the forward-message you pass back. Indeed, the total number of soldiers is never passed as a message—no one ever says it aloud.

An analogous principle operates in rigorous probabilistic reasoning about causality. If you learn something about whether it's raining, from some source *other* than observing the sidewalk to be wet, this will send a forward-message from $\boxed{\text{Rain}}$ to $\boxed{\text{Sidewalk Wet}}$ and raise our expectation of the sidewalk being wet. If you observe the sidewalk to be wet, this sends a backward-message to our belief that it is raining, and this message propagates from $\boxed{\text{Rain}}$ to all neighboring nodes *except* the $\boxed{\text{Sidewalk Wet}}$ node. We count each piece of evidence exactly once; no update message ever "bounces" back and forth. The exact algorithm may be found in Judea Pearl's classic *Probabilistic Reasoning in Intelligent Systems: Networks of Plausible Inference*.

So what went wrong in phlogiston theory? When we observe that fire is hot and bright, the $\boxed{\text{Fire Hot and Bright}}$ node can send backward-evidence to the Phlogiston node, leading us to update our beliefs about phlogiston. But if so, we can't count this as a successful forward-prediction of phlogiston theory. The message should go in only one direction, and not bounce back.

Alas, human beings do not use a rigorous algorithm for updating belief networks. We learn about parent nodes from observing children, and predict child nodes from beliefs about parents. But we don't keep rigorously separate books for the backward-message and forward-message. We just remember that phlogiston is hot, which *causes* fire to be hot. So it seems like phlogiston theory predicts the hotness of fire. Or, worse, it just feels like *phlogiston makes the fire hot.*

Until you notice that no *advance* predictions are being made, the non-constraining causal node is not labeled "fake." It's represented the same way as any other node in your belief network. It feels like a fact, like all the other facts you know: *Phlogiston makes the fire hot.*

A properly designed AI would notice the problem instantly. This wouldn't even require special-purpose code, just correct bookkeeping of the belief network. (Sadly, we humans can't rewrite our own code, the way a properly designed AI could.)

Speaking of "hindsight bias" is just the nontechnical way of saying that humans do not rigorously separate forward and backward messages, allowing forward messages to be contaminated by backward ones.

Those who long ago went down the path of phlogiston were not trying to be fools. No scientist deliberately wants to get stuck in a blind alley. Are there any fake explanations in *your* mind? If there are, I guarantee they're not labeled "fake explanation," so polling your thoughts for the "fake" keyword will not turn them up.

Thanks to hindsight bias, it's also not enough to check how well your theory "predicts" facts you already know. You've got to predict for tomorrow, not yesterday. It's the only way a messy human mind can be guaranteed of sending a pure forward message.

* 35 *

Semantic Stopsigns

And the child asked:

Q: Where did this rock come from?

A: I chipped it off the big boulder, at the center of the village.

Q: Where did the boulder come from?

A: It probably rolled off the huge mountain that towers over our village.

Q: Where did the mountain come from?

A: The same place as all stone: it is the bones of Ymir, the primordial giant.

Q: Where did the primordial giant, Ymir, come from?

A: From the great abyss, Ginnungagap.

Q: Where did the great abyss, Ginnungagap, come from?

A: Never ask that question.

Consider the seeming paradox of the First Cause. Science has traced events back to the Big Bang, but why did the Big Bang happen? It's all well and good to say that the zero of time begins at the Big Bang—that there is nothing before the Big Bang in the ordinary flow of minutes and hours. But saying this presumes our physical law, which itself appears highly structured; it calls out for explanation. Where did the physical laws come from? You could say that we're all a computer simulation, but then the computer simulation is running on some other world's laws of physics—where did *those* laws of physics come from?

At this point, some people say, "God!"

What could possibly make anyone, even a highly religious person, think this even *helped* answer the paradox of the First Cause? Why wouldn't you automatically ask, "Where did God come from?" Saying "God is uncaused" or "God created Himself" leaves us in exactly the same position as "Time began with the Big Bang." We just ask why the whole metasystem exists in the first place, or why some events but not others are allowed to be uncaused.

My purpose here is not to discuss the seeming paradox of the First Cause, but to ask why anyone would think "God!" *could* resolve the paradox. Saying "God!" is a way of belonging to a tribe, which gives people a motive to say it as often as possible—some people even say it for questions like "Why did this hurricane strike New Orleans?" Even so, you'd hope people would notice that on the *particular* puzzle of the First Cause, saying "God!" doesn't help. It doesn't make the paradox seem any less paradoxical *even if true*. How could anyone *not* notice this?

Jonathan Wallace suggested that "God!" functions as a semantic stopsign—that it isn't a propositional assertion, so much as a cognitive traffic signal: do not think past this point.[1] Saying "God!" doesn't so much resolve the paradox, as put up a cognitive traffic signal to halt the obvious continuation of the question-and-answer chain.

Of course *you'd* never do that, being a good and proper atheist, right? But "God!" isn't the *only* semantic stopsign, just the obvious first example.

The transhuman technologies—molecular nanotechnology, advanced biotech, genetech, artificial intelligence, et cetera—pose tough policy questions. What kind of role, if any, should a government take in supervising a parent's choice of genes for their child? Could parents deliberately choose genes for schizophrenia? If enhancing a child's intelligence is expensive, should governments help ensure access, to prevent the emergence of a cognitive elite? You can propose various institutions to answer these policy

---

[1] See Wallace's "God vs. God" (http://www.spectacle.org/yearzero/godvgod.html) and "God as a Semantical Signpost" (http://www.spectacle.org/1095/stop1.html).

questions—for example, that private charities should provide financial aid for intelligence enhancement—but the obvious next question is, "Will this institution be effective?" If we rely on product liability lawsuits to prevent corporations from building harmful nanotech, will that really *work*?

I know someone whose answer to every one of these questions is "Liberal democracy!" That's it. That's his answer. If you ask the obvious question of "How well have liberal democracies performed, historically, on problems this tricky?" or "What if liberal democracy does something stupid?" then you're an autocrat, or libertopian, or otherwise a very very bad person. No one is allowed to question democracy.

I once called this kind of thinking "the divine right of democracy." But it is more precise to say that "Democracy!" functioned for him as a semantic stopsign. If anyone had said to him "Turn it over to the Coca-Cola corporation!" he would have asked the obvious next questions: "Why? What will the Coca-Cola corporation do about it? Why should we trust them? Have they done well in the past on equally tricky problems?"

Or suppose that someone says, "Mexican-Americans are plotting to remove all the oxygen in Earth's atmosphere." You'd probably ask, "Why would they do *that*? Don't Mexican-Americans have to breathe too? Do Mexican-Americans even function as a unified conspiracy?" If you don't ask these obvious next questions when someone says, "Corporations are plotting to remove Earth's oxygen," then "Corporations!" functions for you as a semantic stopsign.

Be careful here not to create a new generic counterargument against things you don't like—"Oh, it's just a stopsign!" No word is a stopsign of itself; the question is whether a word has that effect on a particular person. Having strong emotions about something doesn't qualify it as a stopsign. I'm not exactly fond of terrorists or fearful of private property; that doesn't mean "Terrorists!" or "Capitalism!" are cognitive traffic signals unto me. (The word "intelligence" did once have that effect on me, though no longer.) What distinguishes a semantic stopsign is *failure to consider the obvious next question*.

· 36 ·

Mysterious Answers to Mysterious Questions

Imagine looking at your hand, and knowing nothing of cells, nothing of biochemistry, nothing of DNA. You've learned some anatomy from dissection, so you know your hand contains muscles; but you don't know why muscles move instead of lying there like clay. Your hand is just . . . stuff . . . and for some reason it moves under your direction. Is this not magic?

> It seemed to me then, and it still seems to me, most probable
> that the animal body does not act as a thermodynamic engine . . .
> The influence of animal or vegetable life on matter is infinitely
> beyond the range of any scientific inquiry hitherto entered on.
> Its power of directing the motions of moving particles, in the
> demonstrated daily miracle of our human free-will, and in the
> growth of generation after generation of plants from a single
> seed, are infinitely different from any possible result of the
> fortuitous concourse of atoms[.][1]

> [C]onsciousness teaches every individual that they are, to some
> extent, subject to the direction of his will. It appears, therefore,
> that animated creatures have the power of immediately apply-
> ing, to certain moving particles of matter within their bodies,
> forces by which the motions of these particles are directed to
> produce desired mechanical effects.[2]

---

[1] Kelvin, "On the Dissipation of Energy," 1894.

[2] Kelvin, "On the Mechanical action of Heat or Light: On the Power of Animated Creatures over Matter: On the Sources available to Man for the production of Mechanical Effect," 1852.

> Modern biologists are coming once more to a firm acceptance of something beyond mere gravitational, chemical, and physical forces; and that unknown thing is a vital principle.[3]
>
> —Lord Kelvin

This was the theory of *vitalism*; that the mysterious difference between living matter and non-living matter was explained by an *élan vital* or *vis vitalis*. *Élan vital* infused living matter and caused it to move as consciously directed. *Élan vital* participated in chemical transformations which no mere non-living particles could undergo—Wöhler's later synthesis of urea, a component of urine, was a major blow to the vitalistic theory because it showed that mere *chemistry* could duplicate a product of biology.

Calling "élan vital" an explanation, even a fake explanation like phlogiston, is probably giving it too much credit. It functioned primarily as a curiosity-stopper. You said "Why?" and the answer was "Élan vital!"

When you say "Élan vital!" it *feels* like you know why your hand moves. You have a little causal diagram in your head that says:

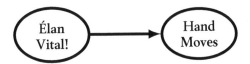

But actually you know nothing you didn't know before. You don't know, say, whether your hand will generate heat or absorb heat, unless you have observed the fact already; if not, you won't be able to predict it in advance. Your curiosity feels sated, but it hasn't been fed. Since you can say "Why? Élan vital!" to any possible observation, it is equally good at explaining all outcomes, a disguised hypothesis of maximum entropy, et cetera.

But the greater lesson lies in the vitalists' reverence for the *élan vital*, their eagerness to pronounce it a mystery beyond all science. Meeting the great dragon Unknown, the vitalists did not draw their swords to do battle,

---

3 Thompson, *The Life of Lord Kelvin*, 2005.

but bowed their necks in submission. They took pride in their ignorance, made biology into a *sacred* mystery, and thereby became loath to relinquish their ignorance when evidence came knocking.

The Secret of Life was *infinitely beyond the reach of science!* Not just a *little* beyond, mind you, but *infinitely* beyond! Lord Kelvin sure did get a tremendous emotional kick out of *not knowing something.*

But ignorance exists in the map, not in the territory. If I am ignorant about a phenomenon, that is a fact about my own state of mind, not a fact about the phenomenon itself. A phenomenon can *seem* mysterious to some particular person. There are no phenomena which are mysterious of themselves. To worship a phenomenon because it seems so wonderfully mysterious is to worship your own ignorance.

Vitalism shared with phlogiston the error of *encapsulating the mystery as a substance.* Fire was mysterious, and the phlogiston theory encapsulated the mystery in a mysterious substance called "phlogiston." Life was a sacred mystery, and vitalism encapsulated the sacred mystery in a mysterious substance called "élan vital." Neither answer helped concentrate the model's probability density—helped make some outcomes easier to explain than others. The "explanation" just wrapped up the question as a small, hard, opaque black ball.

In a comedy written by Moliére, a physician explains the power of a soporific by saying that it contains a "dormitive potency." Same principle. It is a failure of human psychology that, faced with a mysterious phenomenon, we more readily postulate mysterious inherent substances than complex underlying processes.

But the deeper failure is supposing that an *answer* can be mysterious. If a phenomenon feels mysterious, that is a fact about our state of knowledge, not a fact about the phenomenon itself. The vitalists saw a mysterious gap in their knowledge, and postulated a mysterious stuff that plugged the gap. In doing so, they mixed up the map with the territory. All confusion and bewilderment exist in the mind, not in encapsulated substances.

Mysterious Answers to Mysterious Questions

This is the ultimate and fully general explanation for why, again and again in humanity's history, people are shocked to discover that an incredibly mysterious question has a non-mysterious answer. Mystery is a property of questions, not answers.

Therefore I call theories such as vitalism *mysterious answers to mysterious questions*.

These are the signs of mysterious answers to mysterious questions:

- First, the explanation acts as a curiosity-stopper rather than an anticipation-controller.

- Second, the hypothesis has no moving parts—the model is not a specific complex mechanism, but a blankly solid substance or force. The mysterious substance or mysterious force may be said to be here or there, to cause this or that; but the reason why the mysterious force behaves thus is wrapped in a blank unity.

- Third, those who proffer the explanation cherish their ignorance; they speak proudly of how the phenomenon defeats ordinary science or is unlike merely mundane phenomena.

- Fourth, *even after the answer is given, the phenomenon is still a mystery* and possesses the same quality of wonderful inexplicability that it had at the start.

The Futility of Emergence

The failures of phlogiston and vitalism are historical hindsight. Dare I step out on a limb, and name some *current* theory which I deem analogously flawed?

I name *emergence* or *emergent phenomena*—usually defined as the study of systems whose high-level behaviors arise or "emerge" from the interaction of many low-level elements. (Wikipedia: "The way complex systems and patterns arise out of a multiplicity of relatively simple interactions.")

Taken literally, that description fits every phenomenon in our universe above the level of individual quarks, which is part of the problem. Imagine pointing to a market crash and saying "It's not a quark!" Does that feel like an explanation? No? Then neither should saying "It's an emergent phenomenon!"

It's the noun "emergence" that I protest, rather than the verb "emerges from." There's nothing wrong with saying "*X* emerges from *Y*," where *Y* is some specific, detailed model with internal moving parts. "Arises from" is another legitimate phrase that means exactly the same thing. Gravity arises from the curvature of spacetime, according to the specific mathematical model of General Relativity. Chemistry arises from interactions between atoms, according to the specific model of quantum electrodynamics.

Now suppose I should say that gravity depends on "arisence" or that chemistry is an "arising phenomenon," and claim that as my explanation.

The phrase "emerges from" is acceptable, just like "arises from" or "is caused by" are acceptable, if the phrase precedes some specific model to be judged on its own merits.

The Futility of Emergence

However, this is *not* the way "emergence" is commonly used. "Emergence" is commonly used as an explanation in its own right.

I have lost track of how many times I have heard people say, "Intelligence is an emergent phenomenon!" as if that explained intelligence. This usage fits all the checklist items for a mysterious answer to a mysterious question. What do you know, after you have said that intelligence is "emergent"? You can make no new predictions. You do not know anything about the behavior of real-world minds that you did not know before. It feels like you believe a new fact, but you don't anticipate any different outcomes. Your curiosity feels sated, but it has not been fed. The hypothesis has no moving parts—there's no detailed internal model to manipulate. Those who proffer the hypothesis of "emergence" confess their ignorance of the internals, and take pride in it; they contrast the science of "emergence" to other sciences merely mundane.

And even after the answer of "Why? Emergence!" is given, *the phenomenon is still a mystery* and possesses the same sacred impenetrability it had at the start.

A fun exercise is to eliminate the adjective "emergent" from any sentence in which it appears, and see if the sentence says anything different:

- *Before:* Human intelligence is an emergent product of neurons firing.

- *After:* Human intelligence is a product of neurons firing.

- *Before:* The behavior of the ant colony is the emergent outcome of the interactions of many individual ants.

- *After:* The behavior of the ant colony is the outcome of the interactions of many individual ants.

- *Even better:* A colony is made of ants. We can successfully predict some aspects of colony behavior using models that include only individual ants, without any global colony variables, showing that we understand how those colony behaviors arise from ant behaviors.

Another fun exercise is to replace the word "emergent" with the old word, the explanation that people had to use before emergence was invented:

- *Before:* Life is an emergent phenomenon.

- *After:* Life is a magical phenomenon.

- *Before:* Human intelligence is an emergent product of neurons firing.

- *After:* Human intelligence is a magical product of neurons firing.

Does not each statement convey exactly the same amount of knowledge about the phenomenon's behavior? Does not each hypothesis fit exactly the same set of outcomes?

"Emergence" has become very popular, just as saying "magic" used to be very popular. "Emergence" has the same deep appeal to human psychology, for the same reason. "Emergence" is such a wonderfully easy explanation, and it feels good to say it; it gives you a sacred mystery to worship. Emergence is popular *because* it is the junk food of curiosity. You can explain anything using emergence, and so people do just that; for it feels so wonderful to explain things.

Humans are still humans, even if they've taken a few science classes in college. Once they find a way to escape the shackles of settled science, they get up to the same shenanigans as their ancestors—dressed up in the literary genre of "science," but humans are still humans, and human psychology is still human psychology.

· 38 ·

Say Not "Complexity"

Once upon a time . . .

This is a story from when I first met Marcello, with whom I would later work for a year on AI theory; but at this point I had not yet accepted him as my apprentice. I knew that he competed at the national level in mathematical and computing olympiads, which sufficed to attract my attention for a closer look; but I didn't know yet if he could learn to think about AI.

I had asked Marcello to say how he thought an AI might discover how to solve a Rubik's Cube. Not in a preprogrammed way, which is trivial, but rather how the AI itself might figure out the laws of the Rubik universe and reason out how to exploit them. How would an AI *invent for itself* the concept of an "operator," or "macro," which is the key to solving the Rubik's Cube?

At some point in this discussion, Marcello said: "Well, I think the AI needs complexity to do X, and complexity to do Y—"

And I said, "Don't say '*complexity*.'"

Marcello said, "Why not?"

I said, "Complexity should never be a goal in itself. You may need to use a particular algorithm that adds some amount of complexity, but complexity for the sake of complexity just makes things harder." (I was thinking of all the people whom I had heard advocating that the Internet would "wake up" and become an AI when it became "sufficiently complex.")

And Marcello said, "But there's got to be *some* amount of complexity that does it."

I closed my eyes briefly, and tried to think of how to explain it all in words. To me, saying "complexity" simply *felt* like the wrong move in the

AI dance. No one can think fast enough to deliberate, in words, about each sentence of their stream of consciousness; for that would require an infinite recursion. We think in words, but our stream of consciousness is steered below the level of words, by the trained-in remnants of past insights and harsh experience . . .

I said, "Did you read 'A Technical Explanation of Technical Explanation'?"[1]

"Yes," said Marcello.

"Okay," I said. "Saying 'complexity' doesn't concentrate your probability mass."

"Oh," Marcello said, "like 'emergence.' Huh. So . . . now I've got to think about how X might actually happen . . ."

That was when I thought to myself, "*Maybe **this** one is teachable.*"

Complexity is not a useless concept. It has mathematical definitions attached to it, such as Kolmogorov complexity and Vapnik-Chervonenkis complexity. Even on an intuitive level, complexity is often worth thinking about—you have to judge the complexity of a hypothesis and decide if it's "too complicated" given the supporting evidence, or look at a design and try to make it simpler.

But concepts are not useful or useless of themselves. Only *usages* are correct or incorrect. In the step Marcello was trying to take in the dance, he was trying to explain something for free, get something for nothing. It is an extremely common misstep, at least in my field. You can join a discussion on artificial general intelligence and watch people doing the same thing, left and right, over and over again—constantly skipping over things they don't understand, without realizing that's what they're doing.

In an eyeblink it happens: putting a non-controlling causal node behind something mysterious, a causal node that feels like an explanation but isn't. The mistake takes place below the level of words. It requires no special

---

[1]Link: http://lesswrong.com/rationality/a-technical-explanation-of-technical-explanation.

character flaw; it is how human beings think by default, how they have thought since the ancient times.

What you must avoid is *skipping over the mysterious part*; you must linger at the mystery to confront it directly. There are many words that can skip over mysteries, and some of them would be legitimate in other contexts— "complexity," for example. But the essential mistake is that *skip-over*, regardless of what causal node goes behind it. The skip-over is not a thought, but a microthought. You have to pay close attention to catch yourself at it. And when you train yourself to avoid skipping, it will become a matter of instinct, not verbal reasoning. You have to *feel* which parts of your map are still blank, and more importantly, pay attention to that feeling.

I suspect that in academia there is a huge pressure to sweep problems under the rug so that you can present a paper with the appearance of completeness. You'll get more kudos for a seemingly complete model that includes some "emergent phenomena," versus an explicitly incomplete map where the label says "I got no clue how this part works" or "then a miracle occurs." A journal may not even accept the latter paper, since who knows but that the unknown steps are really where everything interesting happens?[2]

And if you're working on a revolutionary AI startup, there is an even huger pressure to sweep problems under the rug; or you will have to admit to yourself that you don't know how to build the right kind of AI yet, and your current life plans will come crashing down in ruins around your ears. But perhaps I am over-explaining, since skip-over happens by default in humans. If you're looking for examples, just watch people discussing religion or philosophy or spirituality or any science in which they were not professionally trained.

---

[2] And yes, it sometimes happens that all the non-magical parts of your map turn out to also be non-important. That's the price you sometimes pay, for entering into terra incognita and trying to solve problems *incrementally*. But that makes it even *more* important to *know* when you aren't finished yet. Mostly, people don't dare to enter terra incognita at all, for the deadly fear of wasting their time.

Marcello and I developed a convention in our AI work: when we ran into something we didn't understand, which was often, we would say "magic"—as in, X magically does Y"—to remind ourselves that *here was an unsolved problem, a gap in our understanding.* It is far better to say "magic" than "complexity" or "emergence"; the latter words create an illusion of understanding. Wiser to say "magic," and leave yourself a placeholder, a reminder of work you will have to do later.

39

Positive Bias: Look into the Dark

I am teaching a class, and I write upon the blackboard three numbers: 2-4-6. "I am thinking of a rule," I say, "which governs sequences of three numbers. The sequence 2-4-6, as it so happens, obeys this rule. Each of you will find, on your desk, a pile of index cards. Write down a sequence of three numbers on a card, and I'll mark it 'Yes' for fits the rule, or 'No' for not fitting the rule. Then you can write down another set of three numbers and ask whether it fits again, and so on. When you're confident that you know the rule, write down the rule on a card. You can test as many triplets as you like."

Here's the record of one student's guesses:

4-6-2	No
4-6-8	Yes
10-12-14	Yes .

At this point the student wrote down their guess at the rule. What do *you* think the rule is? Would you have wanted to test another triplet, and if so, what would it be? Take a moment to think before continuing.

The challenge above is based on a classic experiment due to Peter Wason, the 2-4-6 task. Although subjects given this task typically expressed high confidence in their guesses, only 21% of the subjects successfully guessed the experimenter's real rule, and replications since then have continued to show success rates of around 20%.

The study was called "On the failure to eliminate hypotheses in a conceptual task." Subjects who attempt the 2-4-6 task usually try to generate *positive* examples, rather than *negative* examples—they apply the hypothetical rule to generate a representative instance, and see if it is labeled "Yes."

Thus, someone who forms the hypothesis "numbers increasing by two" will test the triplet 8-10-12, hear that it fits, and confidently announce the rule. Someone who forms the hypothesis X-$2X$-$3X$ will test the triplet 3-6-9, discover that it fits, and then announce that rule.

In every case the actual rule is the same: the three numbers must be in ascending order.

But to discover this, you would have to generate triplets that *shouldn't* fit, such as 20-23-26, and see if they are labeled "No." Which people tend not to do, in this experiment. In some cases, subjects devise, "test," and announce rules far more complicated than the actual answer.

This cognitive phenomenon is usually lumped in with "confirmation bias." However, it seems to me that the phenomenon of trying to test *positive* rather than *negative* examples, ought to be distinguished from the phenomenon of trying to preserve the belief you started with. "Positive bias" is sometimes used as a synonym for "confirmation bias," and fits this particular flaw much better.

It once seemed that phlogiston theory could explain a flame going out in an enclosed box (the air became saturated with phlogiston and no more could be released). But phlogiston theory could just as well have explained the flame *not* going out. To notice this, you have to search for negative examples instead of positive examples, look into zero instead of one; which goes against the grain of what experiment has shown to be human instinct.

For by instinct, we human beings only live in half the world.

One may be lectured on positive bias for days, and yet overlook it in-the-moment. Positive bias is not something we do as a matter of logic, or even as a matter of emotional attachment. The 2-4-6 task is "cold," logical, not affectively "hot." And yet the mistake is sub-verbal, on the level of imagery, of instinctive reactions. Because the problem doesn't arise from following a deliberate rule that says "Only think about positive examples," it can't be solved just by knowing verbally that "We ought to think about both positive and negative examples." Which example automatically pops into your head? You have to learn, wordlessly, to zag instead of zig. You have to learn to flinch toward the zero, instead of away from it.

I have been writing for quite some time now on the notion that the strength of a hypothesis is what it *can't* explain, not what it *can*—if you are equally good at explaining any outcome, you have zero knowledge. So to spot an explanation that isn't helpful, it's not enough to think of what it does explain very well—you also have to search for results it *couldn't* explain, and this is the true strength of the theory.

So I said all this, and then I challenged the usefulness of "emergence" as a concept. One commenter cited superconductivity and ferromagnetism as examples of emergence. I replied that non-superconductivity and non-ferromagnetism were also examples of emergence, which was the problem. But be it far from me to criticize the commenter! Despite having read extensively on "confirmation bias," I didn't spot the "gotcha" in the 2-4-6 task the first time I read about it. It's a subverbal blink-reaction that has to be retrained. I'm still working on it myself.

So much of a rationalist's skill is below the level of words. It makes for challenging work in trying to convey the Art through words. People will agree with you, but then, in the next sentence, do something subdeliberative that goes in the opposite direction. Not that I'm complaining! A major reason I'm writing this is to observe what my words *haven't* conveyed.

Are you searching for positive examples of positive bias right now, or sparing a fraction of your search on what positive bias should lead you to *not* see? Did you look toward light or darkness?

40

Lawful Uncertainty

In *Rational Choice in an Uncertain World,* Robyn Dawes describes an experiment by Tversky:[1]

> Many psychological experiments were conducted in the late
> 1950s and early 1960s in which subjects were asked to predict
> the outcome of an event that had a random component but yet
> had base-rate predictability—for example, subjects were asked
> to predict whether the next card the experimenter turned over
> would be red or blue in a context in which 70% of the cards
> were blue, but in which the sequence of red and blue cards was
> totally random.
>
> In such a situation, the strategy that will yield the highest
> proportion of success is to predict the more common event. For
> example, if 70% of the cards are blue, then predicting blue on
> every trial yields a 70% success rate.
>
> What subjects tended to do instead, however, was match
> probabilities—that is, predict the more probable event with the
> relative frequency with which it occurred. For example, subjects
> tended to predict 70% of the time that the blue card would
> occur and 30% of the time that the red card would occur. Such a
> strategy yields a 58% success rate, because the subjects are correct
> 70% of the time when the blue card occurs (which happens with
> probability .70) and 30% of the time when the red card occurs

---

[1]Tversky and Edwards, "Information versus Reward in Binary Choices," 1966. See also Schul and Mayo, "Searching for Certainty in an Uncertain World," 2003.

(which happens with probability .30); (.70 × .70) + (.30 × .30) = .58.

In fact, subjects predict the more frequent event with a slightly higher probability than that with which it occurs, but do not come close to predicting its occurrence 100% of the time, even when they are paid for the accuracy of their predictions . . . For example, subjects who were paid a nickel for each correct prediction over a thousand trials . . . predicted [the more common event] 76% of the time.

Do not think that this experiment is about a minor flaw in gambling strategies. It compactly illustrates the most important idea in all of rationality.

Subjects just keep guessing red, as if they think they have some way of predicting the random sequence. Of this experiment Dawes goes on to say, "Despite feedback through a thousand trials, subjects cannot bring themselves to believe that the situation is one in which they *cannot* predict."

But the error must go deeper than that. Even if subjects *think* they've come up with a hypothesis, they don't have to *actually bet* on that prediction in order to test their hypothesis. They can say, "Now if *this* hypothesis is correct, the next card will be red"—and then just bet on blue. They can pick blue each time, accumulating as many nickels as they can, while mentally noting their private guesses for any patterns they thought they spotted. If their predictions come out right, *then* they can switch to the newly discovered sequence.

I wouldn't fault a subject for continuing to invent hypotheses—how could they know the sequence is truly beyond their ability to predict? But I would fault a subject for *betting on the guesses*, when this wasn't necessary to gather information, and literally *hundreds* of earlier guesses had been disconfirmed.

Can even a human be *that* overconfident?

I would suspect that something simpler is going on—that the all-blue strategy *just didn't occur* to the subjects.

People see a mix of mostly blue cards with some red, and suppose that the optimal betting strategy must be a mix of mostly blue cards with some red.

It is a *counterintuitive* idea that, given incomplete information, *the optimal betting strategy does not resemble a typical sequence of cards.*

It is a *counterintuitive* idea that the optimal strategy is to behave lawfully, even in an environment that has random elements.

It seems like your behavior ought to be unpredictable, just like the environment—but no! *A random key does not open a random lock just because they are "both random."*

You don't fight fire with fire; you fight fire with water. But this thought involves an extra step, a new concept not directly activated by the problem statement, and so it's not the first idea that comes to mind.

In the dilemma of the blue and red cards, our partial knowledge tells us—on each and every round—that the best bet is blue. This advice of our partial knowledge is the same on every single round. If 30% of the time we go against our partial knowledge and bet on red instead, then we will do worse thereby—because now we're being outright stupid, betting on what we know is the less probable outcome.

If you bet on red every round, you would do as badly as you could possibly do; you would be 100% stupid. If you bet on red 30% of the time, faced with 30% red cards, then you're making yourself 30% stupid.

When your knowledge is incomplete—meaning that the world will seem to you to have an element of randomness—randomizing your actions doesn't solve the problem. Randomizing your actions takes you further from the target, not closer. In a world already foggy, throwing away your intelligence just makes things worse.

It is a *counterintuitive* idea that the optimal strategy can be to *think lawfully, even under conditions of uncertainty.*

And so there are not many rationalists, for most who perceive a chaotic world will try to fight chaos with chaos. You have to take an extra step, and think of something that doesn't pop right into your mind, in order to imagine fighting fire with something that is not itself fire.

You have heard the unenlightened ones say, "Rationality works fine for dealing with rational people, but the world isn't rational." But *faced with an irrational opponent, throwing away your own reason is not going to help you.* There are lawful forms of thought that still generate the best response, even when faced with an opponent who breaks those laws. Decision theory does *not* burst into flames and die when faced with an opponent who disobeys decision theory.

This is no more obvious than the idea of betting all blue, faced with a sequence of both blue and red cards. But each bet that you make on red is an expected loss, and so too with every departure from the Way in your own thinking.

How many *Star Trek* episodes are thus refuted? How many theories of AI?

41

My Wild and Reckless Youth

It is said that parents do all the things they tell their children not to do, which is how they know not to do them.

Long ago, in the unthinkably distant past, I was a devoted Traditional Rationalist, conceiving myself skilled according to that kind, yet I knew not the Way of Bayes. When the young Eliezer was confronted with a mysterious-seeming question, the precepts of Traditional Rationality did not stop him from devising a Mysterious Answer. It is, by far, the most embarrassing mistake I made in my life, and I still wince to think of it.

What was my mysterious answer to a mysterious question? This I will not describe, for it would be a long tale and complicated. I was young, and a mere Traditional Rationalist who knew not the teachings of Tversky and Kahneman. I knew about Occam's Razor, but not the conjunction fallacy. I thought I could get away with thinking complicated thoughts myself, in the literary style of the complicated thoughts I read in science books, not realizing that correct complexity is only possible when every step is pinned down overwhelmingly. Today, one of the chief pieces of advice I give to aspiring young rationalists is "Do not attempt long chains of reasoning or complicated plans."

Nothing more than this need be said: even after I invented my "answer," the phenomenon was still a mystery unto me, and possessed the same quality of wondrous impenetrability that it had at the start.

Make no mistake, that younger Eliezer was not stupid. All the errors of which the young Eliezer was guilty are still being made today by respected scientists in respected journals. It would have taken a subtler skill to protect him than ever he was taught as a Traditional Rationalist.

Indeed, the young Eliezer diligently and painstakingly followed the injunctions of Traditional Rationality in the course of going astray.

As a Traditional Rationalist, the young Eliezer was careful to ensure that his Mysterious Answer made a bold prediction of future experience. Namely, I expected future neurologists to discover that neurons were exploiting quantum gravity, a la Sir Roger Penrose. This required neurons to maintain a certain degree of quantum coherence, which was something you could look for, and find or not find. Either you observe that or you don't, right?

But my hypothesis made no *retrospective* predictions. According to Traditional Science, retrospective predictions don't count—so why bother making them? To a Bayesian, on the other hand, if a hypothesis does not *today* have a favorable likelihood ratio over "I don't know," it raises the question of why you *today* believe anything more complicated than "I don't know." But I knew not the Way of Bayes, so I was not thinking about likelihood ratios or focusing probability density. I had Made a Falsifiable Prediction; was this not the Law?

As a Traditional Rationalist, the young Eliezer was careful not to believe in magic, mysticism, carbon chauvinism, or anything of that sort. I proudly professed of my Mysterious Answer, "It is just physics like all the rest of physics!" As if you could save magic from being a cognitive isomorph of magic, by calling it quantum gravity. But I knew not the Way of Bayes, and did not see the level on which my idea was isomorphic to magic. I gave my *allegiance* to physics, but this did not save me; what does probability theory know of allegiances? I avoided everything that Traditional Rationality told me was forbidden, but what was left was still magic.

Beyond a doubt, my allegiance to Traditional Rationality helped me get out of the hole I dug myself into. If I hadn't been a Traditional Rationalist, I would have been *completely* screwed. But Traditional Rationality still wasn't enough to get it *right*. It just led me into different mistakes than the ones it had explicitly forbidden.

When I think about how my younger self very carefully followed the rules of Traditional Rationality in the course of getting the answer *wrong*, it sheds light on the question of why people who call themselves "rationalists" do not rule the world. You need *one whole hell of a lot* of rationality before it does anything but lead you into new and interesting mistakes.

Traditional Rationality is taught as an art, rather than a science; you read the biography of famous physicists describing the lessons life taught them, and you try to do what they tell you to do. But you haven't lived their lives, and half of what they're trying to describe is an instinct that has been trained into them.

The way Traditional Rationality is designed, it would have been acceptable for me to spend thirty years on my silly idea, so long as I succeeded in falsifying it eventually, and was honest with myself about what my theory predicted, and accepted the disproof when it arrived, et cetera. This is enough to let the Ratchet of Science click forward, but it's a little harsh on the people who waste thirty years of their lives. Traditional Rationality is a walk, not a dance. It's designed to get you to the truth *eventually*, and gives you all too much time to smell the flowers along the way.

Traditional Rationalists can agree to disagree. Traditional Rationality doesn't have the *ideal* that thinking is an exact art in which there is only one correct probability estimate given the evidence. In Traditional Rationality, you're allowed to guess, and then test your guess. But experience has taught me that if you don't *know*, and you guess, you'll end up being wrong.

The Way of Bayes is also an imprecise art, at least the way I'm holding forth upon it. These essays are still fumbling attempts to put into words lessons that would be better taught by experience. But at least there's *underlying* math, plus experimental evidence from cognitive psychology on how humans actually think. Maybe that will be enough to cross the stratospherically high threshold required for a discipline that lets you actually get it right, instead of just constraining you into interesting new mistakes.

• 42 •

Failing to Learn from History

Once upon a time, in my reckless youth, when I knew not the Way of Bayes, I gave a Mysterious Answer to a mysterious-seeming question. Many failures occurred in sequence, but one mistake stands out as most critical: My younger self did not realize that *solving a mystery should make it feel less confusing.* I was trying to explain a Mysterious Phenomenon—which to me meant providing a cause for it, fitting it into an integrated model of reality. Why should this make the phenomenon less Mysterious, when that is its nature? I was trying to *explain* the Mysterious Phenomenon, not render it (by some impossible alchemy) into a mundane phenomenon, a phenomenon that wouldn't even call out for an unusual explanation in the first place.

As a Traditional Rationalist, I knew the historical tales of astrologers and astronomy, of alchemists and chemistry, of vitalists and biology. But the Mysterious Phenomenon was not like this. It was something *new,* something stranger, something more difficult, something that ordinary science had failed to explain for centuries—

—as if stars and matter and life had not been mysteries for hundreds of years and thousands of years, from the dawn of human thought right up until science finally solved them—

We learn about astronomy and chemistry and biology in school, and it seems to us that these matters have *always been* the proper realm of science, that they have *never been* mysterious. When science dares to challenge a new Great Puzzle, the children of that generation are skeptical, for they have never seen science explain something that *feels* mysterious to them.

Science is only good for explaining *scientific* subjects, like stars and matter and life.

I thought the lesson of history was that astrologers and alchemists and vitalists had an innate character flaw, a tendency toward mysterianism, which led them to come up with mysterious explanations for non-mysterious subjects. But surely, if a phenomenon really *was* very weird, a weird explanation might be in order?

It was only afterward, when I began to see the mundane structure inside the mystery, that I realized whose shoes I was standing in. Only then did I realize how reasonable vitalism had seemed *at the time*, how *surprising* and *embarrassing* had been the universe's reply of, "Life is mundane, and does not need a weird explanation."

We read history but we don't *live* it, we don't *experience* it. If only I had *personally* postulated astrological mysteries and then discovered Newtonian mechanics, postulated alchemical mysteries and then discovered chemistry, postulated vitalistic mysteries and then discovered biology. I would have thought of my Mysterious Answer and said to myself: *No way am I falling for that again.*

Making History Available

There is a habit of thought which I call the *logical fallacy of generalization from fictional evidence*. Journalists who, for example, talk about the *Terminator* movies in a report on AI, do not usually treat *Terminator* as a prophecy or fixed truth. But the movie is recalled—is available—as if it were an illustrative historical case. As if the journalist had seen it happen on some other planet, so that it might well happen here.

There is an inverse error to generalizing from fictional evidence: failing to be sufficiently moved by *historical* evidence. The trouble with generalizing from fictional evidence is that it is fiction—it never actually happened. It's not drawn from the same distribution as this, our real universe; fiction differs from reality in systematic ways. But history *has* happened, and *should* be available.

In our ancestral environment, there were no movies; what you saw with your own eyes was true. Is it any wonder that fictions we see in lifelike moving pictures have too great an impact on us? Conversely, things that *really happened*, we encounter as ink on paper; they happened, but we never *saw* them happen. We don't remember them happening to us.

The inverse error is to treat history as mere story, process it with the same part of your mind that handles the novels you read. You may say with your lips that it is "truth," rather than "fiction," but that doesn't mean you are being moved as much as you should be. Many biases involve being insufficiently moved by dry, abstract information.

When I finally realized whose shoes I was standing in, after having given a Mysterious Answer to a mysterious question, there was a sudden shock of unexpected connection with the past. I realized that the invention and destruction of vitalism—which I had only read about in books—had *actually happened to real people*, who experienced it much the same way I experienced the invention and destruction of my own mysterious answer. And I also realized that if I had actually *experienced* the past—if I had lived through past scientific revolutions myself, rather than reading about them in history books—I probably would *not* have made the same mistake again. I would not have come up with *another* mysterious answer; the first thousand lessons would have hammered home the moral.

So (I thought), to feel sufficiently the force of history, I should try to approximate the thoughts of an Eliezer who *had* lived through history— I should try to think as if everything I read about in history books had actually happened to me.[1] I should immerse myself in history, imagine *living* through eras I only saw as ink on paper.

Why should I remember the Wright Brothers' first flight? I was not there. But as a rationalist, could I dare to *not* remember, when the event actually happened? Is there so much difference between seeing an event through your eyes—which is actually a causal chain involving reflected photons, not a direct connection—and seeing an event through a history book? Photons and history books both descend by causal chains from the event itself.

I had to overcome the false amnesia of being born at a particular time. I had to recall—make available—*all* the memories, not just the memories which, by mere coincidence, belonged to myself and my own era.

The Earth became older, of a sudden.

To my former memory, the United States had always existed—there was never a time when there was no United States. I had not remembered, until that time, how the Roman Empire rose, and brought peace and order, and lasted through so many centuries, until I forgot that things had ever been otherwise; and yet the Empire fell, and barbarians overran my city, and the

---

[1] With appropriate reweighting for the availability bias of history books—I should remember being a thousand peasants for every ruler.

learning that I had possessed was lost. The modern world became more fragile to my eyes; it was not the first modern world.

So many mistakes, made over and over and *over* again, because I did not remember making them, in every era I never lived . . .

And to think, people sometimes wonder if overcoming bias is important.

Don't you remember how many times your biases have killed you? You don't? I've noticed that sudden amnesia often follows a fatal mistake. But take it from me, it happened. I remember; I wasn't there.

So the next time you doubt the strangeness of the future, remember how you were born in a hunter-gatherer tribe ten thousand years ago, when no one knew of Science at all. Remember how you were shocked, to the depths of your being, when Science explained the great and terrible sacred mysteries that you once revered so highly. Remember how you once believed that you could fly by eating the right mushrooms, and then you accepted with disappointment that you would never fly, and then you flew. Remember how you had always thought that slavery was right and proper, and then you changed your mind. Don't imagine how you *could* have predicted the change, for that is amnesia. *Remember* that, in fact, you did not guess. Remember how, century after century, the world changed in ways you did not guess.

Maybe then you will be less shocked by what happens next.

44

Explain/Worship/Ignore?

As our tribe wanders through the grasslands, searching for fruit trees and prey, it happens every now and then that water pours down from the sky.

"Why does water sometimes fall from the sky?" I ask the bearded wise man of our tribe.

He thinks for a moment, this question having never occurred to him before, and then says, "From time to time, the sky spirits battle, and when they do, their blood drips from the sky."

"Where do the sky spirits come from?" I ask.

His voice drops to a whisper. "From the before time. From the long long ago."

When it rains, and you don't know why, you have several options. First, you could simply not ask why—not follow up on the question, or never think of the question in the first place. This is the Ignore command, which the bearded wise man originally selected. Second, you could try to devise some sort of explanation, the Explain command, as the bearded man did in response to your first question. Third, you could enjoy the sensation of mysteriousness—the Worship command.

Now, as you are bound to notice from this story, each time you select Explain, the best-case scenario is that you get an explanation, such as "sky spirits." But then this explanation itself is subject to the same dilemma—Explain, Worship, or Ignore? Each time you hit Explain, science grinds for a while, returns an explanation, and then another dialog box pops up. As good rationalists, we feel duty-bound to keep hitting Explain, but it seems like a road that has no end.

You hit Explain for life, and get chemistry; you hit Explain for chemistry, and get atoms; you hit Explain for atoms, and get electrons and nuclei; you hit Explain for nuclei, and get quantum chromodynamics and quarks; you hit Explain for how the quarks got there, and get back the Big Bang . . .

We can hit Explain for the Big Bang, and wait while science grinds through its process, and maybe someday it will return a perfectly good explanation. But then that will just bring up another dialog box. So, if we continue long enough, we must come to a *special* dialog box, a *new* option, an Explanation That Needs No Explanation, a place where the chain ends—and this, maybe, is the only explanation worth knowing.

There—I just hit Worship.

Never forget that there are many more ways to worship something than lighting candles around an altar.

If I'd said, "Huh, that does seem paradoxical. I wonder how the apparent paradox is resolved?" then I would have hit Explain, which does sometimes take a while to produce an answer.

And if the whole issue seems to you unimportant, or irrelevant, or if you'd rather put off thinking about it until tomorrow, than you have hit Ignore.

Select your option wisely.

45

"Science" as Curiosity-Stopper

Imagine that I, in full view of live television cameras, raised my hands and chanted *abracadabra* and caused a brilliant light to be born, flaring in empty space beyond my outstretched hands. Imagine that I committed this act of blatant, unmistakeable sorcery under the full supervision of James Randi and all skeptical armies. Most people, I think, would be *fairly curious* as to what was going on.

But now suppose instead that I don't go on television. I do not wish to share the power, nor the truth behind it. I want to keep my sorcery secret. And yet I also want to cast my spells whenever and wherever I please. I want to cast my brilliant flare of light so that I can read a book on the train—without anyone becoming curious. Is there a spell that stops curiosity?

Yes indeed! Whenever anyone asks "How did you do that?" I just say "Science!"

It's not a real explanation, so much as a curiosity-stopper. It doesn't tell you whether the light will brighten or fade, change color in hue or saturation, and it certainly doesn't tell you how to make a similar light yourself. You don't actually *know* anything more than you knew before I said the magic word. But you turn away, satisfied that nothing unusual is going on.

Better yet, the same trick works with a standard light switch.

Flip a switch and a light bulb turns on. Why?

In school, one is taught that the password to the light bulb is "Electricity!" By now, I hope, you're wary of marking the light bulb "understood" on such a basis. Does saying "Electricity!" let you do calculations that will control your anticipation of experience? There is, at the least, a great deal more to learn.[1]

If you thought the light bulb was *scientifically inexplicable*, it would seize the *entirety* of your attention. You would drop whatever else you were doing, and focus on that light bulb.

But what does the phrase "scientifically explicable" mean? It means that someone *else* knows how the light bulb works. When you are told the light bulb is "scientifically explicable," you don't know more than you knew earlier; you don't know whether the light bulb will brighten or fade. But because someone *else* knows, it devalues the knowledge in your eyes. You become less curious.

Someone is bound to say, "If the light bulb were unknown to science, you could gain fame and fortune by investigating it." But I'm not talking about greed. I'm not talking about career ambition. I'm talking about the raw emotion of curiosity—the feeling of being intrigued. Why should *your* curiosity be diminished because someone *else*, not you, knows how the light bulb works? Is this not spite? It's not enough for *you* to know; other people must also be ignorant, or you won't be happy?

There are goods that knowledge may serve besides curiosity, such as the social utility of technology. For these instrumental goods, it matters whether some other entity in local space already knows. But for my own curiosity, why should it matter?

Besides, consider the consequences if you permit "Someone else knows the answer" to function as a curiosity-stopper. One day you walk into your living room and see a giant green elephant, seemingly hovering in midair, surrounded by an aura of silver light.

"What the heck?" you say.

And a voice comes from above the elephant, saying,

SOMEBODY ALREADY KNOWS WHY THIS ELEPHANT IS HERE.

---

[1] Physicists should ignore this paragraph and substitute a problem in evolutionary theory, where the substance of the theory is again in calculations that few people know how to perform.

"Science" as Curiosity-Stopper

"Oh," you say, "in that case, never mind," and walk on to the kitchen.

I don't know the grand unified theory for this universe's laws of physics. I also don't know much about human anatomy with the exception of the brain. I couldn't point out on my body where my kidneys are, and I can't recall offhand what my liver does.[2]

Should I, so far as *curiosity* is concerned, be more intrigued by my ignorance of the ultimate laws of physics, than the fact that I don't know much about what goes on inside my own body?

If I raised my hands and cast a light spell, you would be intrigued. Should you be any *less* intrigued by the very fact that I raised my hands? When you raise your arm and wave a hand around, this act of will is coordinated by (among other brain areas) your cerebellum. I bet you don't know how the cerebellum works. *I* know a little—though only the gross details, not enough to perform calculations . . . but so what? What does that matter, if *you* don't know? Why should there be a double standard of curiosity for sorcery and hand motions?

Look at yourself in the mirror. Do you know what you're looking at? Do you know what looks out from behind your eyes? Do you know what you are? Some of that answer Science knows, and some of it Science does not. But why should that distinction matter to your curiosity, if *you* don't know?

Do you know how your knees work? Do you know how your shoes were made? Do you know why your computer monitor glows? Do you know why water is wet?

The world around you is full of puzzles. Prioritize, if you must. But do not complain that cruel Science has emptied the world of mystery. With reasoning such as that, I could get you to overlook an elephant in your living room.

---

[2] I am not proud of this. Alas, with all the math I need to study, I'm not likely to learn anatomy anytime soon.

Truly Part of You

A classic paper by Drew McDermott, "Artificial Intelligence Meets Natural Stupidity," criticized AI programs that would try to represent notions like *happiness is a state of mind* using a semantic network:

```
STATE-OF-MIND
     ∧
     | IS-A
     |
 HAPPINESS
```

And of course there's nothing *inside* the HAPPINESS node; it's just a naked LISP token with a suggestive English name.

So, McDermott says, "A good test for the disciplined programmer is to try using gensyms in key places and see if he still admires his system. For example, if STATE-OF-MIND is renamed G1073 . . ." then we would have IS-A(HAPPINESS, G1073) "which looks much more dubious."

Or as I would slightly rephrase the idea: If you substituted randomized symbols for *all* the suggestive English names, you would be completely unable to figure out what G1071(G1072, G1073) meant. Was the AI program meant to represent hamburgers? Apples? Happiness? Who knows? *If you delete the suggestive English names, they don't grow back.*

Suppose a physicist tells you that "Light is waves," and you *believe* the physicist. You now have a little network in your head that says:

IS-A(LIGHT, WAVES).

If someone asks you "What is light made of?" you'll be able to say "Waves!"

As McDermott says, "The whole problem is getting the hearer to notice what it has been told. Not 'understand,' but 'notice.'" Suppose that instead the physicist told you, "Light is made of little curvy things."[1] Would you *notice* any difference of anticipated experience?

How can you realize that you shouldn't trust your seeming knowledge that "light is waves"? One test you could apply is asking, "Could I *regenerate* this knowledge if it were somehow deleted from my mind?"

This is similar in spirit to scrambling the names of suggestively named LISP tokens in your AI program, and seeing if someone else can figure out what they allegedly "refer" to. It's also similar in spirit to observing that an Artificial Arithmetician programmed to record and play back

$$\text{Plus-Of(Seven, Six) = Thirteen}$$

can't regenerate the knowledge if you delete it from memory, until another human re-enters it in the database. Just as if you forgot that "light is waves," you couldn't get back the knowledge except the same way you got the knowledge to begin with—by asking a physicist. You couldn't generate the knowledge for yourself, the way that physicists originally generated it.

The same experiences that lead us to formulate a belief, connect that belief to other knowledge and sensory input and motor output. If you see a beaver chewing a log, then you know what this thing-that-chews-through-logs looks like, and you will be able to recognize it on future occasions whether it is called a "beaver" or not. But if you acquire your beliefs about beavers by someone else telling you facts about "beavers," you may not be able to recognize a beaver when you see one.

This is the terrible danger of trying to *tell* an artificial intelligence facts that it could not learn for itself. It is also the terrible danger of trying to *tell* someone about physics that they cannot verify for themselves. For what physicists mean by "wave" is not "little squiggly thing" but a purely mathematical concept.

---

[1] Not true, by the way.

As Donald Davidson observes, if you believe that "beavers" live in deserts, are pure white in color, and weigh 300 pounds when adult, then you do not have any beliefs *about* beavers, true or false. Your belief about "beavers" is not right enough to be wrong.[2] If you don't have enough experience to regenerate beliefs when they are deleted, then do you have enough experience to connect that belief to anything at all? Wittgenstein: "A wheel that can be turned though nothing else moves with it, is not part of the mechanism."

Almost as soon as I started reading about AI—even before I read McDermott—I realized it would be *a really good idea* to always ask myself: "How would I regenerate this knowledge if it were deleted from my mind?"

The deeper the deletion, the stricter the test. If all proofs of the Pythagorean Theorem were deleted from my mind, could I re-prove it? I think so. If all knowledge of the Pythagorean Theorem were deleted from my mind, would I notice the Pythagorean Theorem to re-prove? That's harder to boast, without putting it to the test; but if you handed me a right triangle with sides of length 3 and 4, and told me that the length of the hypotenuse was calculable, I think I would be able to calculate it, if I still knew all the rest of my math.

What about the notion of *mathematical proof*? If no one had ever told it to me, would I be able to reinvent *that* on the basis of other beliefs I possess? There was a time when humanity did not have such a concept. Someone must have invented it. What was it that they noticed? Would I notice if I saw something equally novel and equally important? Would I be able to think that far outside the box?

How much of your knowledge could you regenerate? From how deep a deletion? It's not just a test to cast out insufficiently connected beliefs. It's a way of absorbing *a fountain of knowledge, not just one fact*.

---

[2] Rorty, "Out of the Matrix: How the Late Philosopher Donald Davidson Showed That Reality Can't Be an Illusion," 2003, http://archive.boston.com/news/globe/ideas/articles/2003/10/05/out_of_the_matrix/.

Truly Part of You

A shepherd builds a counting system that works by throwing a pebble into a bucket whenever a sheep leaves the fold, and taking a pebble out whenever a sheep returns. If you, the apprentice, do not understand this system—if it is magic that works for no apparent reason—then you will not know what to do if you accidentally drop an extra pebble into the bucket. That which you cannot make yourself, you cannot *remake* when the situation calls for it. You cannot go back to the source, tweak one of the parameter settings, and regenerate the output, without the source. If "two plus four equals six" is a brute fact unto you, and then one of the elements changes to "five," how are you to know that "two plus five equals seven" when you were simply *told* that "two plus four equals six"?

If you see a small plant that drops a seed whenever a bird passes it, it will not occur to you that you can use this plant to partially automate the sheep-counter. Though you learned something that the original maker would use to improve on their invention, you can't go back to the source and re-create it.

When you contain the source of a thought, that thought can change along with you as you acquire new knowledge and new skills. When you contain the source of a thought, it becomes truly a part of you and grows along with you.

Strive to make yourself the source of every thought worth thinking. If the thought originally came from outside, make sure it comes from inside as well. Continually ask yourself: "How would I regenerate the thought if it were deleted?" When you have an answer, imagine *that* knowledge being deleted as well. And when you find a fountain, see what else it can pour.

Postlude:
The Simple Truth

The Simple Truth

I remember this paper I wrote on existentialism. My teacher gave it back with an F. She'd underlined true and truth wherever it appeared in the essay, probably about twenty times, with a question mark beside each. She wanted to know what I meant by truth.

—Danielle Egan, journalist

This essay is meant to restore a naive view of truth.

Someone says to you: "My miracle snake oil can rid you of lung cancer in just three weeks." You reply: "Didn't a clinical study show this claim to be untrue?" The one returns: "This notion of 'truth' is quite naive; what do you mean by 'true'?"

Many people, so questioned, don't know how to answer in exquisitely rigorous detail. Nonetheless they would not be wise to abandon the concept of "truth." There was a time when no one knew the equations of gravity in exquisitely rigorous detail, yet if you walked off a cliff, you would fall.

Often I have seen—especially on Internet mailing lists—that amidst other conversation, someone says "X is true," and then an argument breaks out over the use of the word "true." This essay is *not* meant as an encyclopedic reference for that argument. Rather, I hope the arguers will read this essay, and then go back to whatever they were discussing before someone questioned the nature of truth.

In this essay I pose questions. If you see what seems like a really obvious answer, it's probably the answer I intend. The obvious choice isn't *always* the best choice, but sometimes, by golly, it *is*. I don't stop looking as soon

Postlude

I find an obvious answer, but if I go on looking, and the obvious-seeming answer *still* seems obvious, I don't feel guilty about keeping it. Oh, sure, everyone *thinks* two plus two is four, everyone *says* two plus two is four, and in the mere mundane drudgery of everyday life everyone *behaves* as if two plus two is four, but what does two plus two *really, ultimately* equal? As near as I can figure, four. It's still four even if I intone the question in a solemn, portentous tone of voice.

Does that seem like an unduly simple answer? Maybe, on this occasion, life doesn't *need* to be complicated. Wouldn't that be refreshing?

If you are one of those fortunate folk to whom the question seems trivial at the outset, I hope it still seems trivial at the finish. If you find yourself stumped by deep and meaningful questions, remember that if you know exactly how a system works, and could build one yourself out of buckets and pebbles, it should not be a mystery to you.

If confusion threatens when you interpret a metaphor as a metaphor, try taking everything *completely literally.*

Imagine that in an era before recorded history or formal mathematics, I am a shepherd and I have trouble tracking my sheep. My sheep sleep in an enclosure, a fold; and the enclosure is high enough to guard my sheep from wolves that roam by night. Each day I must release my sheep from the fold to pasture and graze; each night I must find my sheep and return them to the fold. If a sheep is left outside, I will find its body the next morning, killed and half-eaten by wolves. But it is so discouraging, to scour the fields for hours, looking for one last sheep, when I know that probably all the sheep are in the fold. Sometimes I give up early, and usually I get away with it; but around a tenth of the time there is a dead sheep the next morning.

If only there were some way to divine whether sheep are still grazing, without the inconvenience of looking! I try several methods: I toss the divination sticks of my tribe; I train my psychic powers to locate sheep through clairvoyance; I search carefully for reasons to believe all the sheep are in the fold. It makes no difference. Around a tenth of the times I turn in early, I find a dead sheep the next morning. Perhaps I realize that my methods aren't working, and perhaps I carefully excuse each failure; but my dilemma is still the same. I can spend an hour searching every possible nook and cranny, when most of the time there are no remaining sheep; or I can go to sleep early and lose, on the average, one-tenth of a sheep.

Late one afternoon I feel especially tired. I toss the divination sticks and the divination sticks say that all the sheep have returned. I visualize each nook and cranny, and I don't imagine scrying any sheep. I'm still not confident enough, so I look inside the fold and it seems like there are a lot of sheep, and I review my earlier efforts and decide that I was especially diligent. This dissipates my anxiety, and I go to sleep. The next morning I discover *two* dead sheep. Something inside me snaps, and I begin thinking creatively.

That day, loud hammering noises come from the gate of the sheepfold's enclosure.

The next morning, I open the gate of the enclosure only a little way, and as each sheep passes out of the enclosure, I drop a pebble into a bucket nailed up next to the door. In the afternoon, as each returning sheep passes by, I take one pebble out of the bucket. When there are no pebbles left in the bucket, I can stop searching and turn in for the night. It is a *brilliant* notion. It will revolutionize shepherding.

That was the theory. In practice, it took considerable refinement before the method worked reliably. Several times I searched for hours and didn't find any sheep, and the next morning there were no stragglers. On each of these occasions it required deep thought to figure out where my bucket system had failed. On returning from one fruitless search, I thought back and realized that the bucket already contained pebbles when I started; this, it turned out, was a bad idea. Another time I randomly tossed pebbles into the bucket, to amuse myself, between the morning and the afternoon;

this too was a bad idea, as I realized after searching for a few hours. But I practiced my pebblecraft, and became a reasonably proficient pebblecrafter.

One afternoon, a man richly attired in white robes, leafy laurels, sandals, and business suit trudges in along the sandy trail that leads to my pastures.

"Can I help you?" I inquire.

The man takes a badge from his coat and flips it open, proving beyond the shadow of a doubt that he is Markos Sophisticus Maximus, a delegate from the Senate of Rum. (One might wonder whether another could steal the badge; but so great is the power of these badges that if any other were to use them, they would in that instant be *transformed* into Markos.)

"Call me Mark," he says. "I'm here to confiscate the magic pebbles, in the name of the Senate; artifacts of such great power must not fall into ignorant hands."

"That bleedin' apprentice," I grouse under my breath, "he's been yakkin' to the villagers again." Then I look at Mark's stern face, and sigh. "They aren't magic pebbles," I say aloud. "Just ordinary stones I picked up from the ground."

A flicker of confusion crosses Mark's face, then he brightens again. "I'm here for the magic bucket!" he declares.

"It's not a magic bucket," I say wearily. "I used to keep dirty socks in it."

Mark's face is puzzled. "Then where is the magic?" he demands.

An interesting question. "It's hard to explain," I say.

My current apprentice, Autrey, attracted by the commotion, wanders over and volunteers his explanation: "It's the level of pebbles in the bucket," Autrey says. "There's a magic level of pebbles, and you have to get the level just right, or it doesn't work. If you throw in more pebbles, or take some out, the bucket won't be at the magic level anymore. Right now, the magic level is," Autrey peers into the bucket, "about one-third full."

"I see!" Mark says excitedly. From his back pocket Mark takes out his own bucket, and a heap of pebbles. Then he grabs a few handfuls of pebbles, and stuffs them into the bucket. Then Mark looks into the bucket, noting how many pebbles are there. "There we go," Mark says, "the magic level of this bucket is half full. Like that?"

"No!" Autrey says sharply. "Half full is not the magic level. The magic level is about one-third. Half full is definitely unmagic. Furthermore, you're using the wrong bucket."

Mark turns to me, puzzled. "I thought you said the bucket wasn't magic?"

"It's not," I say. A sheep passes out through the gate, and I toss another pebble into the bucket. "Besides, I'm watching the sheep. Talk to Autrey."

Mark dubiously eyes the pebble I tossed in, but decides to temporarily shelve the question. Mark turns to Autrey and draws himself up haughtily. "It's a free country," Mark says, "under the benevolent dictatorship of the Senate, of course. I can drop whichever pebbles I like into whatever bucket I like."

Autrey considers this. "No you can't," he says finally, "there won't be any magic."

"Look," says Mark patiently, "I watched you carefully. You looked in your bucket, checked the level of pebbles, and called that the magic level. I did exactly the same thing."

"That's not how it works," says Autrey.

"Oh, I see," says Mark, "It's not the level of pebbles in *my* bucket that's magic, it's the level of pebbles in *your* bucket. Is that what you claim? What makes your bucket so much better than mine, huh?"

"Well," says Autrey, "if we were to empty your bucket, and then pour all the pebbles from my bucket into your bucket, then your bucket would have the magic level. There's also a procedure we can use to check if your bucket has the magic level, if we know that my bucket has the magic level; we call that a bucket compare operation."

Another sheep passes, and I toss in another pebble.

"He just tossed in another pebble!" Mark says. "And I suppose you claim the new level is also magic? I could toss pebbles into your bucket until the level was the same as mine, and then our buckets would agree. You're just comparing my bucket to your bucket to determine whether *you* think the level is 'magic' or not. Well, I think *your* bucket isn't magic, because it doesn't have the same level of pebbles as mine. So there!"

"Wait," says Autrey, "you don't understand—"

"By 'magic level,' you mean simply the level of pebbles in your own bucket. And when I say 'magic level,' I mean the level of pebbles in my bucket. Thus you look at my bucket and say it 'isn't magic,' but the word 'magic' means different things to different people. You need to specify *whose* magic it is. You should say that my bucket doesn't have 'Autrey's magic level,' and I say that your bucket doesn't have 'Mark's magic level.' That way, the apparent contradiction goes away."

"But—" says Autrey helplessly.

"Different people can have different buckets with different levels of pebbles, which proves this business about 'magic' is completely arbitrary and subjective."

"Mark," I say, "did anyone tell you what these pebbles *do?*"

"*Do?*" says Mark. "I thought they were just magic."

"If the pebbles didn't do anything," says Autrey, "our ISO 9000 process efficiency auditor would eliminate the procedure from our daily work."

"What's your auditor's name?"

"Darwin," says Autrey.

"Hm," says Mark. "Charles does have a reputation as a strict auditor. So do the pebbles bless the flocks, and cause the increase of sheep?"

"No," I say. "The virtue of the pebbles is this; if we look into the bucket and see the bucket is empty of pebbles, we know the pastures are likewise empty of sheep. If we do not use the bucket, we must search and search until dark, lest one last sheep remain. Or if we stop our work early, then sometimes the next morning we find a dead sheep, for the wolves savage any sheep left outside. If we look in the bucket, we know when all the sheep are home, and we can retire without fear."

Mark considers this. "That sounds rather implausible," he says eventually. "Did you consider using divination sticks? Divination sticks are infallible, or at least, anyone who says they are fallible is burned at the stake. This is an extremely painful way to die, so the divination sticks must be *extremely* infallible."

"You're welcome to use divination sticks if you like," I say.

"Oh, good heavens, of course not," says Mark. "They work infallibly, with absolute perfection on every occasion, as befits such blessed instruments. But what if there were a dead sheep the next morning? I only use the divination sticks when there is no possibility of their being proven wrong. Otherwise I might be burned alive. So how does your magic bucket work?"

How does the bucket work . . . ? I'd better start with the simplest possible case. "Well," I say, "suppose the pastures are empty, and the bucket isn't empty. Then we'll waste hours looking for a sheep that isn't there. And if there are sheep in the pastures, but the bucket is empty, then Autrey and I will turn in too early, and we'll find dead sheep the next morning. So an empty bucket is magical if and only if the pastures are empty—"

"Hold on," says Autrey. "That sounds like a vacuous tautology to me. Aren't an empty bucket and empty pastures obviously the same thing?"

"It's not vacuous," I say. "Here's an analogy: The logician Alfred Tarski once said that the assertion 'Snow is white' is true if and only if snow is white. If you can understand that, you should be able to see why an empty bucket is magical if and only if the pastures are empty of sheep."

"Hold on," says Mark. "These are *buckets*. They don't have anything to do with *sheep*. Buckets and sheep are obviously completely different. There's no way the sheep can ever interact with the bucket."

"Then where do *you* think the magic comes from?" inquires Autrey.

Mark considers. "You said you could compare two buckets to check if they had the same level . . . I can see how buckets can interact with buckets. Maybe when you get a large collection of buckets, and they all have the same level, *that's* what generates the magic. I'll call that the coherentist theory of magic buckets."

"Interesting," says Autrey. "I know that my master is working on a system with multiple buckets—he says it might work better because of 'redundancy' and 'error correction.' That sounds like coherentism to me."

Postlude

"They're not quite the same—" I start to say.

"Let's test the coherentism theory of magic," says Autrey. "I can see you've got five more buckets in your back pocket. I'll hand you the bucket we're using, and then you can fill up your other buckets to the same level—"

Mark recoils in horror. "Stop! These buckets have been passed down in my family for generations, and they've always had the same level! If I accept your bucket, my bucket collection will become less coherent, and the magic will go away!"

"But your *current* buckets don't have anything to do with the sheep!" protests Autrey.

Mark looks exasperated. "Look, I've explained before, there's obviously no way that sheep can interact with buckets. Buckets can only interact with other buckets."

"I toss in a pebble whenever a sheep passes," I point out.

"When a sheep passes, you toss in a pebble?" Mark says. "What does that have to do with anything?"

"It's an interaction between the sheep and the pebbles," I reply.

"No, it's an interaction between the pebbles and *you*," Mark says. "The magic doesn't come from the sheep, it comes from *you*. Mere sheep are obviously nonmagical. The magic has to come from *somewhere*, on the way to the bucket."

I point at a wooden mechanism perched on the gate. "Do you see that flap of cloth hanging down from that wooden contraption? We're still fiddling with that—it doesn't work reliably—but when sheep pass through, they disturb the cloth. When the cloth moves aside, a pebble drops out of a reservoir and falls into the bucket. That way, Autrey and I won't have to toss in the pebbles ourselves."

Mark furrows his brow. "I don't quite follow you . . . is the *cloth* magical?"

I shrug. "I ordered it online from a company called Natural Selections. The fabric is called Sensory Modality." I pause, seeing the incredulous expressions of Mark and Autrey. "I admit the names are a bit New Agey. The point is that a passing sheep triggers a chain of cause and effect that ends with a pebble in the bucket. *Afterward* you can compare the bucket to other buckets, and so on."

"I still don't get it," Mark says. "You can't fit a sheep into a bucket. Only pebbles go in buckets, and it's obvious that pebbles only interact with other pebbles."

"The sheep interact with things that interact with pebbles . . ." I search for an analogy. "Suppose you look down at your shoelaces. A photon leaves the Sun; then travels down through Earth's atmosphere; then bounces off your shoelaces; then passes through the pupil of your eye; then strikes the retina; then is absorbed by a rod or a cone. The photon's energy makes the attached neuron fire, which causes other neurons to fire. A neural activation pattern in your visual cortex can interact with your beliefs about your shoelaces, since beliefs about shoelaces also exist in neural substrate. If you can understand that, you should be able to see how a passing sheep causes a pebble to enter the bucket."

"At exactly *which* point in the process does the pebble become magic?" says Mark.

"It . . . um . . ." Now *I'm* starting to get confused. I shake my head to clear away cobwebs. This all seemed simple enough when I woke up this morning, and the pebble-and-bucket system hasn't gotten any more complicated since then. "This is a lot easier to understand if you remember that the *point* of the system is to keep track of sheep."

Mark sighs sadly. "Never mind . . . it's obvious you don't know. Maybe all pebbles are magical to start with, even before they enter the bucket. We could call that position panpebblism."

"Ha!" Autrey says, scorn rich in his voice. "Mere wishful thinking! Not all pebbles are created equal. The pebbles in *your* bucket are *not* magical. They're only lumps of stone!"

Mark's face turns stern. "Now," he cries, "now you see the danger of the road you walk! Once you say that some people's pebbles are magical and some are not, your pride will consume you! You will think yourself superior to all others, and so fall! Many throughout history have tortured and murdered because they thought their own pebbles supreme!" A tinge of condescension enters Mark's voice. "Worshipping a level of pebbles as 'magical' implies that there's an absolute pebble level in a Supreme Bucket. Nobody believes in a Supreme Bucket these days."

"One," I say. "Sheep are not absolute pebbles. Two, I don't think my bucket actually contains the sheep. Three, I don't worship my bucket level as perfect—I adjust it sometimes—and I do that *because* I care about the sheep."

"Besides," says Autrey, "if someone believes that possessing absolute pebbles *would* license torture and murder, they're making a mistake that has nothing to do with buckets. You're solving the wrong problem."

Mark calms himself down. "I suppose I can't expect any better from mere shepherds. You probably believe that snow is white, don't you."

"Um . . . yes?" says Autrey.

"It doesn't bother you that *Joseph Stalin* believed that snow is white?"

"Um . . . no?" says Autrey.

Mark gazes incredulously at Autrey, and finally shrugs. "Let's suppose, purely for the sake of argument, that your pebbles are magical and mine aren't. Can you tell me what the difference is?"

"My pebbles *represent* the sheep!" Autrey says triumphantly. "*Your* pebbles don't have the representativeness property, so they won't work. They are empty of meaning. Just look at them. There's no aura of semantic content; they are merely pebbles. You need a bucket with special causal powers."

"Ah!" Mark says. "Special causal powers, instead of magic."

"Exactly," says Autrey. "I'm not superstitious. Postulating magic, in this day and age, would be unacceptable to the international shepherding community. We have found that postulating magic simply doesn't work as an explanation for shepherding phenomena. So when I see something I don't understand, and I want to explain it using a model with no internal detail that makes no predictions even in retrospect, I postulate special causal powers. Or I'll call it an emergent phenomenon, or something."

"What kind of special powers does the bucket have?" asks Mark.

"Hm," says Autrey. "Maybe this bucket is imbued with an *about-ness* relation to the pastures. That would explain why it worked—when the bucket is empty, it *means* the pastures are empty."

"Where did you find this bucket?" says Mark. "And how did you realize it had an about-ness relation to the pastures?"

"It's an *ordinary bucket*," I say. "I used to climb trees with it . . . I don't think this question *needs* to be difficult."

"I'm talking to Autrey," says Mark.

"You have to bind the bucket to the pastures, and the pebbles to the sheep, using a magical ritual—pardon me, an emergent process with special causal powers—that my master discovered," Autrey explains.

Autrey then attempts to describe the ritual, with Mark nodding along in sage comprehension.

"You have to throw in a pebble *every* time a sheep leaves through the gate?" says Mark. "Take out a pebble *every* time a sheep returns?"

Autrey nods. "Yeah."

"That must be really hard," Mark says sympathetically.

Autrey brightens, soaking up Mark's sympathy like rain. "Exactly!" says Autrey. "It's *extremely* hard on your emotions. When the bucket has held its level for a while, you . . . tend to get attached to that level."

A sheep passes then, leaving through the gate. Autrey sees; he stoops, picks up a pebble, holds it aloft in the air. "Behold!" Autrey proclaims. "A sheep has passed! I must now toss a pebble into this bucket, my dear bucket, and destroy that fond level which has held for so long—" Another sheep passes. Autrey, caught up in his drama, misses it, so I plunk a pebble into the bucket. Autrey is still speaking: "—for that is the supreme test of the shepherd, to throw in the pebble, be it ever so agonizing, be the old level ever so precious. Indeed, only the best of shepherds can meet a requirement so stern—"

"Autrey," I say, "if you want to be a great shepherd someday, learn to shut up and throw in the pebble. No fuss. No drama. Just do it."

"And this ritual," says Mark, "it binds the pebbles to the sheep by the magical laws of Sympathy and Contagion, like a voodoo doll."

Autrey winces and looks around. "Please! Don't call it Sympathy and Contagion. We shepherds are an anti-superstitious folk. Use the word 'intentionality,' or something like that."

"Can I look at a pebble?" says Mark.

"Sure," I say. I take one of the pebbles out of the bucket, and toss it to Mark. Then I reach to the ground, pick up another pebble, and drop it into the bucket.

Autrey looks at me, puzzled. "Didn't you just mess it up?"

I shrug. "I don't think so. We'll know I messed it up if there's a dead sheep next morning, or if we search for a few hours and don't find any sheep."

"But—" Autrey says.

"I taught you everything *you* know, but I haven't taught you everything *I* know," I say.

Mark is examining the pebble, staring at it intently. He holds his hand over the pebble and mutters a few words, then shakes his head. "I don't sense any magical power," he says. "Pardon me. I don't sense any intentionality."

"A pebble only has intentionality if it's inside a ma—an emergent bucket," says Autrey. "Otherwise it's just a mere pebble."

"Not a problem," I say. I take a pebble out of the bucket, and toss it away. Then I walk over to where Mark stands, tap his hand holding a pebble, and say: "I declare this hand to be part of the magic bucket!" Then I resume my post at the gates.

Autrey laughs. "Now you're just being gratuitously evil."

I nod, for this is indeed the case.

"Is that really going to work, though?" says Autrey.

I nod again, hoping that I'm right. I've done this before with two buckets, and in principle, there should be no difference between Mark's hand and a bucket. Even if Mark's hand is imbued with the *élan vital* that distinguishes live matter from dead matter, the trick should work as well as if Mark were a marble statue.

Mark is looking at his hand, a bit unnerved. "So . . . the pebble has intentionality again, now?"

"Yep," I say. "Don't add any more pebbles to your hand, or throw away the one you have, or you'll break the ritual."

Mark nods solemnly. Then he resumes inspecting the pebble. "I understand now how your flocks grew so great," Mark says. "With the power of this bucket, you could keep on tossing pebbles, and the sheep would keep returning from the fields. You could start with just a few sheep, let them leave, then fill the bucket to the brim before they returned. And if tending so many sheep grew tedious, you could let them all leave, then empty almost all the pebbles from the bucket, so that only a few returned . . . increasing the flocks again when it came time for shearing . . . dear heavens, man! Do you realize the sheer *power* of this ritual you've discovered? I can only imagine the implications; humankind might leap ahead a decade—no, a century!"

"It doesn't work that way," I say. "If you add a pebble when a sheep hasn't left, or remove a pebble when a sheep hasn't come in, that breaks the ritual. The power does not linger in the pebbles, but vanishes all at once, like a soap bubble popping."

Mark's face is terribly disappointed. "Are you sure?"

I nod. "I tried that and it didn't work."

Mark sighs heavily. "And this . . . *math* . . . seemed so powerful and useful until then . . . Oh, well. So much for human progress."

"Mark, it was a *brilliant* idea," Autrey says encouragingly. "The notion didn't occur to me, and yet it's so obvious . . . it would save an *enormous* amount of effort . . . there *must* be a way to salvage your plan! We could try different buckets, looking for one that would keep the magical pow— the intentionality in the pebbles, even without the ritual. Or try other pebbles. Maybe our pebbles just have the wrong properties to have *inherent* intentionality. What if we tried it using stones carved to resemble tiny sheep? Or just write 'sheep' on the pebbles; that might be enough."

"Not going to work," I predict dryly.

Autrey continues. "Maybe we need organic pebbles, instead of silicon pebbles . . . or maybe we need to use expensive gemstones. The price of gemstones doubles every eighteen months, so you could buy a handful of cheap gemstones now, and wait, and in twenty years they'd be really expensive."

"You tried adding pebbles to create more sheep, and it didn't work?" Mark asks me. "What exactly did you do?"

"I took a handful of dollar bills. Then I hid the dollar bills under a fold of my blanket, one by one; each time I hid another bill, I took another paperclip from a box, making a small heap. I was careful not to keep track in my head, so that all I knew was that there were 'many' dollar bills, and 'many' paperclips. Then when all the bills were hidden under my blanket, I added a single additional paperclip to the heap, the equivalent of tossing an extra pebble into the bucket. Then I started taking dollar bills from under the fold, and putting the paperclips back into the box. When I finished, a single paperclip was left over."

"What does that result mean?" asks Autrey.

"It means the trick didn't work. Once I broke ritual by that single mis-step, the power did not linger, but vanished instantly; the heap of paperclips and the pile of dollar bills no longer went empty at the same time."

"You *actually* tried this?" asks Mark.

"Yes," I say, "I actually performed the experiment, to verify that the outcome matched my theoretical prediction. I have a sentimental fondness for the scientific method, even when it seems absurd. Besides, what if I'd been wrong?"

"If it *had* worked," says Mark, "you would have been guilty of counterfeiting! Imagine if everyone did that; the economy would collapse! Everyone would have billions of dollars of currency, yet there would be nothing for money to buy!"

"Not at all," I reply. "By that same logic whereby adding another paperclip to the heap creates another dollar bill, creating another dollar bill would create an additional dollar's worth of goods and services."

Mark shakes his head. "Counterfeiting is still a crime . . . You should not have tried."

"I was *reasonably* confident I would fail."

"Aha!" says Mark. "You *expected* to fail! You didn't *believe* you could do it!"

"Indeed," I admit. "You have guessed my expectations with stunning accuracy."

"Well, that's the problem," Mark says briskly. "Magic is fueled by belief and willpower. If you don't believe you can do it, you can't. You need to change your belief about the experimental result, if we are to change the result itself."

"Funny," I say nostalgically, "that's what Autrey said when I told him about the pebble-and-bucket method. That it was too ridiculous for him to believe, so it wouldn't work for him."

"How did you persuade him?" inquires Mark.

"I told him to shut up and follow instructions," I say, "and when the method worked, Autrey started believing in it."

Mark frowns, puzzled. "That makes no sense. It doesn't resolve the essential chicken-and-egg dilemma."

"Sure it does. The bucket method works whether or not you believe in it."

"That's *absurd!*" sputters Mark. "I don't believe in magic that works whether or not you believe in it!"

"I said that too," chimes in Autrey. "Apparently I was wrong."

Mark screws up his face in concentration. "But . . . if you didn't believe in magic that works whether or not you believe in it, then why did the bucket method work when you didn't believe in it? Did you believe in magic that works whether or not you believe in it whether or not you believe in magic that works whether or not you believe in it?"

Postlude

"I don't . . . *think* so . . ." says Autrey doubtfully.

"Then if you didn't believe in magic that works whether or not you . . . hold on a second, I need to work this out with paper and pencil—" Mark scribbles frantically, looks skeptically at the result, turns the piece of paper upside down, then gives up. "Never mind," says Mark. "Magic is difficult enough for me to comprehend; metamagic is out of my depth."

"Mark, I don't think you understand the art of bucketcraft," I say. "It's not about using pebbles to control sheep. It's about making sheep control pebbles. In this art, it is not necessary to begin by believing the art will work. Rather, first the art works, then one comes to believe that it works."

"Or so you believe," says Mark.

"So I believe," I reply, "*because* it happens to be a fact. The correspondence between reality and my beliefs comes from reality controlling my beliefs, not the other way around."

Another sheep passes, causing me to toss in another pebble.

"Ah! Now we come to the root of the problem," says Mark. "What's this so-called 'reality' business? I understand what it means for a hypothesis to be elegant, or falsifiable, or compatible with the evidence. It sounds to me like calling a belief 'true' or 'real' or 'actual' is merely the difference between saying you believe something, and saying you really really believe something."

I pause. "Well . . ." I say slowly. "Frankly, I'm not entirely sure myself where this 'reality' business comes from. I can't create my own reality in the lab, so I must not understand it yet. But occasionally I believe strongly that something is going to happen, and then something else happens instead. I need a name for whatever-it-is that determines my experimental results, so I call it 'reality'. This 'reality' is somehow separate from even my very best hypotheses. Even when I have a simple hypothesis, strongly supported by all the evidence I know, sometimes I'm still surprised. So I need different names for the thingies that determine my predictions and the thingy that determines my experimental results. I call the former thingies 'belief,' and the latter thingy 'reality.'"

Mark snorts. "I don't even know why I bother listening to this obvious nonsense. Whatever you say about this so-called 'reality,' it is merely another belief. Even your belief that reality precedes your beliefs is a belief. It follows, as a logical inevitability, that reality does not exist; only beliefs exist."

"Hold on," says Autrey, "could you repeat that last part? You lost me with that sharp swerve there in the middle."

"No matter what you say about reality, it's just another belief," explains Mark. "It follows with crushing necessity that there is no reality, only beliefs."

"I see," I say. "The same way that no matter what you eat, you need to eat it with your mouth. It follows that there is no food, only mouths."

"Precisely," says Mark. "Everything that you eat has to be in your mouth. How can there be food that exists outside your mouth? The thought is nonsense, proving that 'food' is an incoherent notion. That's why we're all starving to death; there's no food."

Autrey looks down at his stomach. "But I'm *not* starving to death."

"*Aha!*" shouts Mark triumphantly. "And how did you utter that very objection? With your *mouth*, my friend! With your *mouth*! What better demonstration could you ask that there is no food?"

"*What's this about starvation?*" demands a harsh, rasping voice from directly behind us. Autrey and I stay calm, having gone through this before. Mark leaps a foot in the air, startled almost out of his wits.

Inspector Darwin smiles tightly, pleased at achieving surprise, and makes a small tick on his clipboard.

"Just a metaphor!" Mark says quickly. "You don't need to take away my mouth, or anything like that—"

"*Why* do you need a *mouth* if there is no *food?*" demands Darwin angrily. "*Never mind.* I have no *time* for this *foolishness.* I am here to inspect the *sheep.*"

"Flock's thriving, sir," I say. "No dead sheep since January."

"*Excellent.* I award you 0.12 units of *fitness*. Now what is this *person* doing here? Is he a necessary part of the *operations?*"

"As far as I can see, he would be of more use to the human species if hung off a hot-air balloon as ballast," I say.

"Ouch," says Autrey mildly.

"I do not *care* about the *human species.* Let him speak for *himself.*"

Mark draws himself up haughtily. "This mere *shepherd,*" he says, gesturing at me, "has claimed that there is such a thing as reality. This offends me, for I know with deep and abiding certainty that there is no truth. The concept of 'truth' is merely a stratagem for people to impose their own beliefs on others. Every culture has a different 'truth,' and no culture's 'truth' is superior to any other. This that I have said holds at all times in all places, and I insist that you agree."

"Hold on a second," says Autrey. "If nothing is true, why should I believe you when you say that nothing is true?"

"I didn't say that nothing is true—" says Mark.

"Yes, you did," interjects Autrey, "I heard you."

"—I said that 'truth' is an excuse used by some cultures to enforce their beliefs on others. So when you say something is 'true,' you mean only that it would be advantageous to your own social group to have it believed."

"And this that you have said," I say, "is it true?"

"Absolutely, positively true!" says Mark emphatically. "People create their own realities."

"Hold on," says Autrey, sounding puzzled again, "saying that people create their own realities is, logically, a completely separate issue from saying that there is no truth, a state of affairs I cannot even imagine coherently, perhaps because you still have not explained how exactly it is supposed to work—"

"There you go again," says Mark exasperatedly, "trying to apply your Western concepts of logic, rationality, reason, coherence, and self-consistency."

"Great," mutters Autrey, "now I need to add a *third* subject heading, to keep track of this entirely separate and distinct claim—"

"It's not separate," says Mark. "Look, you're taking the wrong attitude by treating my statements as hypotheses, and carefully deriving their consequences. You need to think of them as fully general excuses, which I apply when anyone says something I don't like. It's not so much a model of how the universe works, as a Get Out of Jail Free card. The *key* is to apply the excuse *selectively*. When I say that there is no such thing as truth, that applies only to *your* claim that the magic bucket works whether or not I believe in it. It does *not* apply to *my* claim that there is no such thing as truth."

"Um . . . why not?" inquires Autrey.

Mark heaves a patient sigh. "Autrey, do you think you're the first person to think of that question? To ask us how our own beliefs can be meaningful if all beliefs are meaningless? That's the same thing many students say when they encounter this philosophy, which, I'll have you know, has many adherents and an extensive literature."

"So what's the answer?" says Autrey.

"We named it the 'reflexivity problem,'" explains Mark.

"But what's the *answer*?" persists Autrey.

Mark smiles condescendingly. "Believe me, Autrey, you're not the first person to think of such a simple question. There's no point in presenting it to us as a triumphant refutation."

"But what's the *actual answer*?"

"Now, I'd like to move on to the issue of how logic kills cute baby seals—"

"*You* are wasting *time*," snaps Inspector Darwin.

"Not to mention, losing track of sheep," I say, tossing in another pebble.

Inspector Darwin looks at the two arguers, both apparently unwilling to give up their positions. "Listen," Darwin says, more kindly now, "I have a simple notion for resolving your dispute. *You* say," says Darwin, pointing to Mark, "that people's beliefs alter their personal realities. And *you* fervently believe," his finger swivels to point at Autrey, "that Mark's beliefs *can't* alter reality. So let Mark believe really hard that he can fly, and then step off a cliff. Mark shall see himself fly away like a bird, and Autrey shall see him plummet down and go splat, and you shall both be happy."

Postlude

We all pause, considering this.

"It *sounds* reasonable . . ." Mark says finally.

"There's a cliff right there," observes Inspector Darwin.

Autrey is wearing a look of intense concentration. Finally he shouts: "Wait! If that were true, we would all have long since departed into our own private universes, in which case the other people here are only figments of your imagination—there's no point in trying to prove anything to us—"

A long dwindling scream comes from the nearby cliff, followed by a dull and lonely splat. Inspector Darwin flips his clipboard to the page that shows the current gene pool and pencils in a slightly lower frequency for Mark's alleles.

Autrey looks slightly sick. "Was that really necessary?"

"*Necessary?*" says Inspector Darwin, sounding puzzled. "It just *happened* . . . I don't quite understand your question."

Autrey and I turn back to our bucket. It's time to bring in the sheep. You wouldn't want to forget about that part. Otherwise what would be the point?

From the *Rationality: From AI to Zombies* Series

Volume 1: Map and Territory

Once upon a time, three groups of subjects were asked how much they would pay to save 2,000 / 20,000 / 200,000 migrating birds from drowning in uncovered oil ponds.

...

Volume 2: How to Actually Change Your Mind

In Orthodox Judaism there is a saying: "The previous generation is to the next one as angels are to men; the next generation is to the previous one as donkeys are to men."

...

Volume 3: The Machine in the Ghost

In our skulls we carry around three pounds of slimy, wet, grayish tissue, corrugated like crumpled toilet paper. You wouldn't think, to look at the unappetizing lump, that it was some of the most powerful stuff in the known universe.

...

Volume 4: Mere Reality

In L. Sprague de Camp's fantasy story *The Incomplete Enchanter*, the hero, Harold Shea, is transported from our own universe into the universe of Norse mythology. This world is based on magic rather than technology; so naturally, when Our Hero tries to light a fire with a match brought along from Earth, the match fails to strike.

...

Volume 5: Mere Goodness

People ask me, "What will artificial intelligences be like? What will they do? Tell us your amazing story about the future."

And lo, I say unto them, "You have asked me a trick question."

...

Volume 6: Becoming Stronger

I once lent Xiaoguang "Mike" Li my copy of *Probability Theory: The Logic of Science.* Mike Li read some of it, and then came back and said:

"Wow...it's like Jaynes is a thousand-year-old vampire."

...

Website: rationalitybook.com

Glossary

a priori   Before considering the evidence. Similarly, "a posteriori" means "after considering the evidence"; compare prior and posterior probabilities.

In philosophy, "a priori" often refers to the stronger idea of something knowable in the absence of *any* experiential evidence (outside of the evidence needed to understand the claim).

anchoring   The cognitive bias of relying excessively on initial information after receiving relevant new information.

anthropics   Problems related to reasoning well about how many observers like you there are.

artificial general intelligence   Artificial intelligence that is "general-purpose" in the same sense that human reasoning is general-purpose. It's hard to crisply state what this kind of reasoning consists in—if we knew how to fully formalize it, we would already know how to build artificial general intelligence. However, we can gesture at (e.g.) humans' ability to excel in many different scientific fields, even though we did not evolve in an ancestral environment containing particle accelerators.

availability heuristic   The tendency to base judgments on how easily relevant examples come to mind.

Bayes's Theorem   The equation stating how to update a hypothesis H in light of new evidence E. In its simplest form, Bayes's Theorem says that a hypothesis' probability given the evidence, written "$P(H|E)$," equals the likelihood of the evidence given that hypothesis, multiplied by your prior probability $P(H)$ that the hypothesis was true, divided by the prior probability $P(E)$ that you would see that evidence regardless. I.e.:

$$P(H|E) = \frac{P(E|H)P(H)}{P(E)} \, .$$

Also known as Bayes's Rule. See "odds ratio" for a simpler way to calculate a Bayesian update.

Bayesian   (a) Optimally reasoned; reasoned in accordance with the laws of probability. (b) An optimal reasoner, or a reasoner that approximates optimal inference unusually well. (c) Someone who treats beliefs as probabilistic and treats probability theory as a relevant ideal for evaluating reasoners. (d) Related to probabilistic belief. (e) Related to Bayesian statistical methods.

Bayesian updating   Revising your beliefs in a way that's fully consistent with the information available to you. Perfect Bayesian updating is wildly intractable in realistic environments, so real-world agents have to rely on imperfect heuristics to get by. As an optimality condition, however, Bayesian updating helps make sense of the idea that some ways of changing one's mind work better than others for learning about the world.

bias   (a) A cognitive bias. In *Rationality: From AI to Zombies*, this will be the default meaning. (b) A statistical bias. (c) An inductive bias. (d) Colloquially: prejudice or unfairness.

bit   (a) A binary digit, taking the value 0 or 1. (b) The logarithm (base 1/2) of a probability—the maximum information that can be communicated using a binary digit, averaged over the digit's states. *Rationality: From AI to Zombies* usually uses "bit" in the latter sense.

Blue and Green   Rival sports teams and political factions in ancient Rome.

calibration   Assigning probabilities to beliefs in a way that matches how often those beliefs turn out to be right. E.g., if your assignment of "70% confidence" to claims is well-calibrated, then you will get such claims right about 70% of the time.

causal decision theory   The theory that the right way to make decisions is by picking the action with the best causal consequences.

cognitive bias   A systematic error stemming from the way human reasoning works. This can be contrasted with errors due to ordinary ignorance, misinformation, brain damage, etc.

conditional probability   The probability that a statement is true on the assumption that some other statement is true. E.g., the conditional probability $P(A|B)$ means "the probability of A given that B."

confirmation bias   The cognitive bias of giving more weight to evidence that agrees with one's current beliefs.

conjunction   A sentence that asserts multiple things. "It's raining *and* I'm eating a sandwich" is a conjunction; its conjuncts are "It's raining" and "I'm eating a sandwich."

conjunction fallacy   The fallacy of treating a conjunction as though it were more likely than its conjuncts.

deontology   The theory that moral conduct is about choosing actions that satisfy specific rules like "don't lie" or "don't steal."

directed acyclic graph   A graph that is directed (its edges have a direction associated with them) and acyclic (there's no way to follow a sequence of edges in a given direction to loop around from a node back to itself).

élan vital   "Vital force." A term coined in 1907 by the philosopher Henri Bergson to refer to a mysterious force that was held to be responsible for life's "aliveness" and goal-oriented behavior.

entanglement   (a) Causal correlation between two things. (b) In quantum physics, the mutual dependence of two particles' states upon one another. Entanglement in sense (b) occurs when a quantum amplitude distribution cannot be factorized.

entropy   (a) In thermodynamics, the number of different ways a physical state may be produced (its Boltzmann entropy). E.g., a slightly shuffled deck has lower entropy than a fully shuffled one, because there are many more configurations a fully shuffled deck is likely to end up in. (b) In information theory, the expected value of the information contained in a message (its Shannon entropy). That is, a random variable's Shannon entropy is how many bits of information one would be missing (on average) if one did not know the variable's value.

Boltzmann entropy and Shannon entropy have turned out to be equivalent; that is, a system's thermodynamic disorder corresponds to the number of bits needed to fully characterize it.

epistemic   Concerning knowledge.

Everett branch   A "world" in the many-worlds interpretation of quantum mechanics.

expected utility   The expected value of a utility function given some action. Roughly: how much an agent's goals will tend to be satisfied by some action, given uncertainty about the action's outcome.

A sure $1 will usually lead to more utility than a 10% chance of $1 million. Yet in all cases, the 10% shot at $1 million has more *expected* utility, assuming you assign more than ten times as much utility to winning $1 million. Expected utility is an idealized mathematical framework for making sense of the idea "good bets don't have to be sure bets."

expected value   The sum of all possible values of a variable, each multiplied by its probability of being the true value.

Fermi Paradox   The puzzle of reconciling "on priors, we should expect there to be many large interstellar civilizations visible in the night sky" and "we see no clear signs of such civilizations."

Some reasons many people find it puzzling that there are no visible alien civilizations include: "the elements required for life on Earth seem commonplace"; "life had billions of years to develop elsewhere before we evolved"; "high intelligence seems relatively easy to evolve (e.g., many of the same cognitive abilities evolved independently in humans, octopuses, crows)"; and "although some goals favor hiddenness, many different possible goals favor large-scale extraction of resources, and we only require there to exist one old species of the latter type."

foozality See "rationality."

graph In graph theory, a mathematical object consisting of simple atomic objects ("vertices," or "nodes") connected by lines (or "edges"). When edges have an associated direction, they are also called "arrows."

hedonic Concerning pleasure.

hindsight bias The tendency to exaggerate how well one could have predicted things that one currently believes.

inductive bias The set of assumptions a leaner uses to derive predictions from a data set. The learner is "biased" in the sense that it's more likely to update in some directions than in others, but unlike with other conceptions of "bias", the idea of "inductive bias" doesn't imply any sort of error.

instrumental Concerning usefulness or effectiveness.

instrumental value A goal that is only pursued in order to further some other goal.

intentionality The ability of things to represent, or refer to, other things. Not to be confused with "intent."

isomorphism A two-way mapping between objects in a category. Informally, two things are often called "isomorphic" if they're identical in every relevant respect.

Kolmogorov complexity   A formalization of the idea of complexity. Given a programming language, a computable string's Kolmogorov complexity is the length of the shortest computer program in that language that outputs the string.

likelihood   In Bayesian probability theory, how much probability a hypothesis assigns to a piece of evidence. Suppose we observe the evidence E = "Mr. Boddy was knifed," and our hypotheses are H_P = "Professor Plum killed Boddy" and H_W = "Mrs. White killed Boddy." If we think there's a 25% chance that Plum would use a knife in the worlds where he chose to kill Boddy, then we can say H_P assigns a likelihood of 25% to E.

Suppose that there's only a 5% chance Mrs. White would use a knife if she killed Boddy. Then we can say that the *likelihood ratio* between H_P and H_W is 25/5 = 5. This means that the evidence supports "Plum did it" five times as strongly as it supports "White did it," which tells us how to update upon observing E. (See "odds ratio" for a simple example.)

magisterium   Stephen Gould's term for a domain where some community or field has authority. Gould claimed that science and religion were separate and non-overlapping magisteria. On his view, religion has authority to answer questions of "ultimate meaning and moral value" (but not empirical fact) and science has authority to answer questions of empirical fact (but not meaning or value).

maximum-entropy probability distribution   A probability distribution which assigns equal probability to every event.

Minimum Message Length Principle   A formalization of Occam's Razor that judges the probability of a hypothesis based on how long it would take to communicate the hypothesis plus the available data. Simpler hypotheses are favored, as are hypotheses that can be used to concisely encode the data.

motivated cognition   Reasoning that is driven by some goal or emotion that's at odds with accuracy. Examples include non-evidence-based inclinations to reject a claim (motivated skepticism), to believe a claim (motivated credulity), to continue evaluating an issue (motivated continuation), or to stop evaluating an issue (motivated stopping).

Murphy's Law   The saying "Anything that can go wrong will go wrong."

mutual information   For two variables, the amount that knowing about one variable tells you about the other's value. If two variables have zero mutual information, then they are independent; knowing the value of one does nothing to reduce uncertainty about the other.

nanotechnology   (a) Fine-grained control of matter on the scale of individual atoms, as in Eric Drexler's writing. This is the default meaning in *Rationality: From AI to Zombies*. (b) Manipulation of matter on a scale of nanometers.

Newcomb's Problem   A central problem in decision theory. Imagine an agent that understands psychology well enough to predict your decisions in advance, and decides to either fill two boxes with money, or fill one box, based on their prediction. They put $1,000 in a transparent box no matter what, and they then put $1 million in an opaque box if (and only if) they predicted that you'd *only* take the opaque box. The predictor tells you about this, and then leaves. Which do you pick?

If you take both boxes ("two-boxing"), you get only the $1000, because the predictor foresaw your choice and didn't fill the opaque box. On the other hand, if you only take the opaque box, you come away with $1 million. So it seems like you should take only the opaque box.

However, *causal decision theorists* object to this strategy on the grounds that you can't causally control what the predictor did in the past; the predictor has already made their decision by the time you make yours, and regardless of whether or not they placed the $1 million in the opaque box, you'll be throwing away a free $1000 if you choose not to take it. For the same reason, causal decision theory prescribes defecting in one-shot Prisoner's Dilemmas, even if you're playing against a perfect atom-by-atom copy of yourself.

normative   Good, or serving as a standard for desirable behavior.

Occam's Razor   The principle that, all else being equal, a simpler claim is more probable than a relatively complicated one. Formalizations of Occam's Razor include Solomonoff induction and the Minimum Message Length Principle.

odds ratio   A way of representing how likely two events are relative to each other. E.g., if I have no information about which day of the week it is, the odds are $1:6$ that it's Sunday. This is the same as saying that "it's Sunday" has a prior probability of 1/7. If $x:y$ is the odds ratio, the probability of x is $x/(x+y)$.

Likewise, to convert a probability p into an odds ratio, I can just write $p:(1-p)$. For a percent probability $p\%$, this becomes $p:(100-p)$. E.g., if my probability of winning a race is 40%, my odds are $40:60$, which can also be written $2:3$.

Odds ratios are useful because they're usually the easiest way to calculate a Bayesian update. If I notice the mall is closing early, and that's twice as likely to happen on a Sunday as it is on a non-Sunday (a likelihood ratio of $2:1$), I can simply multiply the left and right sides of my prior it's Sunday ($1:6$) by the evidence's likelihood ratio ($2:1$) to arrive at a correct posterior probability of $2:6$, or $1:3$.

optimization process   Yudkowsky's term for a process that performs searches through a large search space, and manages to hit very specific targets that would be astronomically unlikely to occur by chance.

E.g., the existence of trees is much easier to understand if we posit a search process, evolution, that iteratively comes up with better and better solutions to cognitively difficult problems. A well-designed dam, similarly, is easier to understand if we posit an optimization process searching for designs or policies that meet some criterion. Evolution, humans, and beavers all share this property, and can therefore be usefully thought of as optimization processes. In contrast, the processes that produce mountains and stars are easiest to describe in other terms.

orthogonality   The independence of two (or more) variables. If two variables are orthogonal, then knowing the value of one doesn't help you learn the value of the other.

phlogiston   A substance hypothesized in the 17th entity to explain phenomena such as fire and rust. Combustible objects were thought by late alchemists and early chemists to contain phlogiston, which evaporated during combustion.

positive bias   Bias toward noticing what a theory predicts you'll see, instead of noticing what a theory predicts you won't see.

posterior probability   An agent's beliefs after acquiring evidence. Contrasted with its prior beliefs, or priors.

prior probability   An agent's beliefs prior to acquiring some evidence.

Prisoner's Dilemma   A game in which each player can choose to either "cooperate" or "defect" with the other. The best outcome for each player is to defect while the other cooperates; and the worst outcome is to cooperate while the other defects. Each player views mutual cooperation as the second-best option, and mutual defection as the second-worst.

Traditionally, game theorists have argued that defection is always the correct move in one-shot dilemmas; it improves your reward if the other player independently cooperates, and it lessens your loss if the other player independently defects.

Yudkowsky is one of a minority of decision theorists who argue that rational cooperation is possible in the one-shot Prisoner's Dilemma, provided the two players' decision-making is known to be sufficiently similar. "My opponent and I are both following the same decision procedure, so if I cooperate, my opponent will cooperate too; and if I defect, my opponent will defect. The former seems preferable, so this decision procedure hereby outputs 'cooperate.'"

probability distribution   A function which assigns a probability (i.e., a number representing how likely something is to be true) to every possibility under consideration. Discrete and continuous probability distributions are generally encoded by, respectively, *probability mass functions* and *probability density functions*.

Thinking of probability as a "mass" that must be divided up between possibilities can be a useful way to keep in view that reducing the probability of one hypothesis always requires increasing the probability of others, and vice versa. Probability, like (classical) mass, is conserved.

quark   An elementary particle of matter.

rationalist   (a) Related to rationality. (b) A person who tries to apply rationality concepts to their real-world decisions.

rationality   Making systematically good decisions (instrumental rationality) and achieving systematically accurate beliefs (epistemic rationality).

representativeness heuristic   A cognitive heuristic where one judges the probability of an event based on how well it matches some mental prototype.

scope insensitivity   A cognitive bias where people tend to disregard the size of certain phenomena.

self-anchoring   Anchoring to oneself. Treating one's own qualities as the default, and only weakly updating toward viewing others as different when given evidence of differences.

Shannon mutual information   See "mutual information."

Solomonoff induction   An attempted definition of optimal (albeit computationally unfeasible) inference. Bayesian updating plus a simplicity prior that assigns less probability to percept-generating programs the longer they are.

Singularity   One of several scenarios in which artificial intelligence systems surpass human intelligence in a large and dramatic way.

statistical bias   A systematic discrepancy between the expected value of some measure, and the true value of the thing you're measuring.

System 1   The processes behind the brain's fast, automatic, emotional, and intuitive judgments.

System 2   The processes behind the brain's slow, deliberative, reflective, and intellectual judgments.

Tegmark world   A universe contained in a vast multiverse of mathematical objects. The idea comes from Max Tegmark's Mathematical Universe Hypothesis, which holds that our own universe is a mathematical object contained in an ensemble in which all possible computable structures exist.

Traditional Rationality   Yudkowsky's term for the scientific norms and conventions espoused by thinkers like Richard Feynman, Carl Sagan, and Charles Peirce. Yudkowsky contrasts this with the ideas of rationality in contemporary mathematics and cognitive science.

truth-value   A proposition's truth or falsity.

Turing machine   An abstract machine that follows rules for manipulating symbols on an arbitrarily long tape.

two-boxing   Taking both boxes in Newcomb's Problem.

updating   Revising one's beliefs. See also "Bayesian updating."

utility function   A function that ranks outcomes by "utility," i.e., by how well they satisfy some set of goals or constraints. Humans are limited and imperfect reasoners, and don't consistently optimize any endorsed utility function; but the idea of optimizing a utility function helps us give formal content to "what it means to pursue a goal well," just as Bayesian updating helps formalize "what it means to learn well."

Bibliography

Baratz, Daphna. *How Justified Is the "Obvious" Reaction?* Stanford University, 1983.

Baron, Jonathan, and Joshua D. Greene. "Determinants of Insensitivity to Quantity in Valuation of Public Goods: Contribution, Warm Glow, Budget Constraints, Availability, and Prominence." *Journal of Experimental Psychology: Applied* 2, no. 2 (1996): 107–125.

Buehler, Roger, Dale Griffin, and Michael Ross. "Exploring the 'Planning Fallacy': Why People Underestimate Their Task Completion Times." *Journal of Personality and Social Psychology* 67, no. 3 (1994): 366–381.

———. "Inside the Planning Fallacy: The Causes and Consequences of Optimistic Time Predictions." In *Heuristics and Biases: The Psychology of Intuitive Judgment,* edited by Thomas Gilovich, Dale Griffin, and Daniel Kahneman, 250–270. New York: Cambridge University Press, 2002.

———. "It's About Time: Optimistic Predictions in Work and Love." *European Review of Social Psychology* 6, no. 1 (1995): 1–32.

Burton, Ian, Robert W. Kates, and Gilbert F. White. *The Environment as Hazard.* 1st ed. New York: Oxford University Press, 1978.

Carson, Richard T., and Robert Cameron Mitchell. "Sequencing and Nesting in Contingent Valuation Surveys." *Journal of Environmental Economics and Management* 28, no. 2 (1995): 155–173.

Combs, Barbara, and Paul Slovic. "Newspaper Coverage of Causes of Death." *Journalism & Mass Communication Quarterly* 56, no. 4 (1979): 837–849.

Dennett, Daniel C. *Breaking the Spell: Religion as a Natural Phenomenon.* Penguin, 2006.

Desvousges, William H., F. Reed Johnson, Richard W. Dunford, Kevin J. Boyle, Sara P. Hudson, and K. Nicole Wilson. *Measuring Nonuse Damages Using Contingent Valuation: An Experimental Evaluation of Accuracy.* Technical report. Research Triangle Park, NC: RTI International, 2010.

Ehrlinger, Joyce, Thomas Gilovich, and Lee Ross. "Peering Into the Bias Blind Spot: People's Assessments of Bias in Themselves and Others." *Personality and Social Psychology Bulletin* 31, no. 5 (2005): 680–692.

Fetherstonhaugh, David, Paul Slovic, Stephen M. Johnson, and James Friedrich. "Insensitivity to the Value of Human Life: A Study of Psychophysical Numbing." *Journal of Risk and Uncertainty* 14, no. 3 (1997): 283–300.

Freire, Paulo. *The Politics of Education: Culture, Power, and Liberation.* Greenwood Publishing Group, 1985.

Gibbon, Edward. *The History of the Decline and Fall of the Roman Empire.* Vol. 4. J. & J. Harper, 1829.

Gilbert, Daniel T., Romin W. Tafarodi, and Patrick S. Malone. "You Can't Not Believe Everything You Read." *Journal of Personality and Social Psychology* 65 (2 1993): 221–233.

Hansen, Katherine, Margaret Gerbasi, Alexander Todorov, Elliott Kruse, and Emily Pronin. "People Claim Objectivity After Knowingly Using Biased Strategies." *Personality and Social Psychology Bulletin* 40, no. 6 (2014): 691–699.

Hanson, Robin. "Beware Value Talk." *Overcoming Bias* (blog), 2009. http://www.overcomingbias.com/2009/02/the-cost-of-talking-values.html.

———. "Policy Tug-O-War." *Overcoming Bias* (blog), 2007. http://www.overcomingbias.com/2007/05/policy_tugowar.html.

Heuer, Richards J. *Psychology of Intelligence Analysis.* Center for the Study of Intelligence, Central Intelligence Agency, 1999.

Holt, Jim. "Thinking Inside the Boxes." *Slate,* 2002. http://www.slate.com/articles/arts/egghead/2002/02/thinkinginside_the_boxes.single.html.

Kahneman, Daniel. "Comments by Professor Daniel Kahneman." In *Valuing Environmental Goods: An Assessment of the Contingent Valuation Method,* edited by Ronald G. Cummings, David S. Brookshire, and William D. Schulze, vol. 1.B, 226–235. Experimental Methods for Assessing Environmental Benefits. Totowa, NJ: Rowman & Allanheld, 1986.

Kahneman, Daniel, and Shane Frederick. "Representativeness Revisited: Attribute Substitution in Intuitive Judgment." In *Heuristics and Biases: The Psychology of Intuitive Judgment,* edited by Thomas Gilovich, Dale Griffin, and Daniel Kahneman. Cambridge University Press, 2002.

Kahneman, Daniel, Ilana Ritov, and David Schkade. "Economic Preferences or Attitude Expressions?: An Analysis of Dollar Responses to Public Issues." *Journal of Risk and Uncertainty* 19, nos. 1–3 (1999): 203–235.

Kelvin, Lord. "On the Dissipation of Energy: Geology and General Physics." In *Popular Lectures and Addresses, vol. ii*. London: Macmillan, 1894.

———. "On the Mechanical action of Heat or Light: On the Power of Animated Creatures over Matter: On the Sources available to Man for the production of Mechanical Effect." *Proceedings of the Royal Society of Edinburgh* 3, no. 1 (1852): 108–113.

Keysar, Boaz. "Language Users as Problem Solvers: Just What Ambiguity Problem Do They Solve?" In *Social and Cognitive Approaches to Interpersonal Communication*, edited by Susan R. Fussell and Roger J. Kreuz, 175–200. Mahwah, NJ: Lawrence Erlbaum Associates, 1998.

———. "The Illusory Transparency of Intention: Linguistic Perspective Taking in Text." *Cognitive Psychology* 26 (2 1994): 165–208.

Keysar, Boaz, and Dale J. Barr. "Self-Anchoring in Conversation: Why Language Users Do Not Do What They 'Should.'" In *Heuristics and Biases: The Psychology of Intuitive Judgment*, edited by Griffin Gilovich and Daniel Kahneman, 150–166. New York: Cambridge University Press, 2002.

Keysar, Boaz, and Bridget Bly. "Intuitions of the Transparency of Idioms: Can One Keep a Secret by Spilling the Beans?" *Journal of Memory and Language* 34 (1 1995): 89–109.

Keysar, Boaz, and Anne S. Henly. "Speakers' Overestimation of Their Effectiveness." *Psychological Science* 13 (3 2002): 207–212.

Kunreuther, Howard, Robin Hogarth, and Jacqueline Meszaros. "Insurer Ambiguity and Market Failure." *Journal of Risk and Uncertainty* 7 (1 1993): 71–87.

Lazarsfeld, Paul F. "The American Solidier—An Expository Review." *Public Opinion Quarterly* 13, no. 3 (1949): 377–404.

Lichtenstein, Sarah, Paul Slovic, Baruch Fischhoff, Mark Layman, and Barbara Combs. "Judged Frequency of Lethal Events." *Journal of Experimental Psychology: Human Learning and Memory* 4, no. 6 (1978): 551–578.

McCluskey, Peter. "Truth Bias." *Overcoming Bias* (blog), 2007. http://www.overcomingbias.com/2007/08/truth-bias.html.

McDermott, Drew. "Artificial Intelligence Meets Natural Stupidity." *SIGART Newsletter*, no. 57 (1976): 4–9.

McFadden, Daniel L., and Gregory K. Leonard. "Issues in the Contingent Valuation of Environmental Goods: Methodologies for Data Collection and Analysis." In *Contingent Valuation: A Critical Assessment*, edited by Jerry A. Hausman, 165–215. Contributions to Economic Analysis 220. New York: North-Holland, 1993.

Meyers, David G. *Exploring Social Psychology*. New York: McGraw-Hill, 1994.

Newby-Clark, Ian R., Michael Ross, Roger Buehler, Derek J. Koehler, and Dale Griffin. "People Focus on Optimistic Scenarios and Disregard Pessimistic Scenarios While Predicting Task Completion Times." *Journal of Experimental Psychology: Applied* 6, no. 3 (2000): 171–182.

Pearl, Judea. *Probabilistic Reasoning in Intelligent Systems: Networks of Plausible Inference*. San Mateo, CA: Morgan Kaufmann, 1988.

Procopius. *History of the Wars*. Edited by Henry B. Dewing. Vol. 1. Harvard University Press, 1914.

Pronin, Emily, Daniel Y. Lin, and Lee Ross. "The Bias Blind Spot: Perceptions of Bias in Self versus Others." *Personality and Social Psychology Bulletin* 28, no. 3 (2002): 369–381.

Rorty, Richard. "Out of the Matrix: How the Late Philosopher Donald Davidson Showed That Reality Can't Be an Illusion." *The Boston Globe*, 2003. http://archive.boston.com/news/globe/ideas/articles/2003/10/05/out_of_the_matrix/.

Sagan, Carl. *The Demon-Haunted World: Science as a Candle in the Dark*. 1st ed. New York: Random House, 1995.

Schul, Yaacov, and Ruth Mayo. "Searching for Certainty in an Uncertain World: The Difficulty of Giving Up the Experiential for the Rational Mode of Thinking." *Journal of Behavioral Decision Making* 16, no. 2 (2003): 93–106.

Serfas, Sebastian. *Cognitive Biases in the Capital Investment Context: Theoretical Considerations and Empirical Experiments on Violations of Normative Rationality*. Springer, 2010.

Tegmark, Max. "Parallel Universes." In *Science and Ultimate Reality: Quantum Theory, Cosmology, and Complexity*, edited by John D. Barrow, Paul C. W. Davies, and Charles L. Harper Jr., 459–491. New York: Cambridge University Press, 2004. http://arxiv.org/abs/astro-ph/0302131.

Thompson, Silvanus Phillips. *The Life of Lord Kelvin*. American Mathematical Society, 2005.

Tversky, Amos, and Ward Edwards. "Information versus Reward in Binary Choices." *Journal of Experimental Psychology* 71, no. 5 (1966): 680–683.

Tversky, Amos, and Daniel Kahneman. "Extensional Versus Intuitive Reasoning: The Conjunction Fallacy in Probability Judgment." *Psychological Review* 90, no. 4 (1983): 293–315.

———. "Judgments of and by Representativeness: Heuristics and Biases." In *Judgment Under Uncertainty*, edited by Daniel Kahneman, Paul Slovic, and Amos Tversky, 84–98. New York: Cambridge University Press, 1982.

Verhagen, Joachim. *Science Jokes*, 2001. http://web.archive.org/web/2006042408293 7/http://www.nvon.nl/scheik/best/diversen/scijokes/scijokes.txt.

Wason, Peter Cathcart. "On the Failure to Eliminate Hypotheses in a Conceptual Task." *Quarterly Journal of Experimental Psychology* 12, no. 3 (1960): 129–140.

Weiten, Wayne. *Psychology: Themes and Variations, Briefer Version, Eighth Edition.* Cengage Learning, 2010.

Wittgenstein, Ludwig. *Philosophical Investigations.* Translated by Gertrude E. M. Anscombe. Oxford: Blackwell, 1953.

Yudkowsky, Eliezer. "Cognitive Biases Potentially Affecting Judgment of Global Risks," edited by Nick Bostrom and Milan M. Ćirković, 91–119. New York: Oxford University Press, 2008.

About the author. Eliezer Yudkowsky is a decision theorist and computer scientist at the Machine Intelligence Research Institute in Berkeley, California who is known for his work in technological forecasting. His publications include the *Cambridge Handbook of Artificial Intelligence* chapter "The Ethics of Artificial Intelligence," co-authored with Nick Bostrom. Yudkowsky's writings have helped spark a number of ongoing academic and public debates about the long-term impact of AI, and he has written a number of popular introductions to topics in cognitive science and formal epistemology, such as *Rationality: From AI to Zombies* and *Harry Potter and the Methods of Rationality*.

Made in the USA
Middletown, DE
27 October 2020

22863947R00128